ESCAPE AND EVASION

ESCAPE AND EVASION

Sqd. Ldr.
Cyril Penna
DFM

Best Wishes

Cyril Penna

UNITED WRITERS
Cornwall

UNITED WRITERS PUBLICATIONS LTD
Ailsa, Castle Gate, Penzance, Cornwall.

British Library Cataloguing in Publication Data
Penna, Cyril
Escape and evasion.
1. World War, 1939-1945—Prisoners
and prisons, German 2. World War,
1939-1945—Personal narratives,
British 3. Escapes
I. Title
940.54'72'430924   D805.F8

ISBN 1 85200 008 2

Printed in Great Britain by
United Writers Publications Ltd
Cornwall

Dedicated to:

The many wonderful friends who made it possible
for me to evade capture.

The medical profession who so carefully and
skilfully nursed me to health.

My wife, Betté, sons Graham and David, their
wives Carol and Rosemary
and
My grandchildren, Lucy, Joseph, Simon and Amy
all of whom have, in various ways, encouraged me
to put on record the events of that fateful journey.

'I said to the man who stood at the gate of the year, "Give me a light that I may tread safely into the unknown."
And he replied, "Go out into the darkness and put your hand in the hand of God. That shall be to you better than light and safer than a known way." '

From *The Desert* by Minnie Louise Haskins, 1908.

I was born in 1922 in a little mining town called Willington, in the County of Durham. My father was a miner and had suffered very badly from wounds he had received in the Great War. He had been savagely bayoneted and left for dead on the battlefield near Arras, in France, along with many others in his Regiment, the Durham Light Infantry. His life had been saved by a cavalryman, who, on seeing him move, lifted him onto his horse and took him to a field hospital. His rescuer turned out to be an inhabitant of a small hamlet some four miles from Willington.

My parents were not wealthy, and as the size of the family grew life became more difficult for work in the colliery became more spasmodic. I remember well the siren that was sounded to tell miners that there was to be no work for the following day. The wailing sound filled the air and, as the weeks passed by, people became more and more despondent, yet somehow the community became more united in its adversity. There can be no doubt that the years of my childhood were hard times for the North East, yet the families survived by a tightening of belts and the produce from the allotment. I cannot remember having a holiday. On occasions I was sent to my grandparents near Durham for a few days, and this period, together with the Sunday School trip was the only change of environment in the year.

As I grew older I was able to supplement the family income by means of the odd sixpence or so that I earned by shovelling coal delivered to the miners' households, as part of their salary, into the coal-houses of the house concerned. This was quite a hard task involving the throwing of the coal by shovelfuls some five feet into a small trapdoor. Often the coals were delivered early in the morning and I would complete the task of 'putting them in' before I left for school. Sometimes I was not able to finish by schooltime if more than one load was delivered, and so I played truant in order to complete the task.

I was unlucky in my schooling in that I not only missed attending because of my desire to help the family finances, but because I was so often ill. I had all the children's ailments imaginable, including scarlet fever and diphtheria. I was very ill with the latter and my life was despaired of but I made a full recovery. Despite the many absences I was a good scholar and having worked hard to catch up soon became one of the star pupils in French language. I recall that my teacher was a very attractive lady and most of the boys in my form would do anything to curry favour.

I cannot say that my childhood was an easy part of my life. In common with most boys at that time I was expected to help with the household chores, the shopping, the gardening and indeed was required to attend Sunday School in the local Methodist Church. There was, of course, no television and most families were not able to afford a radio, so any leisure time was spent attending the various entertainments provided by the Church. Concerts given by local artists were the highlight of the week and were looked forward to with great anticipation. I joined the Boy Scouts and was able to go off to camp and so life became a little more varied.

By the time I had reached fourteen years of age, the fortunes of the family seemed to be improving. I left school and was given a job with the Meadow Dairy, a firm that had a chain of stores throughout the area. My brother, who was three years my senior, was also working and despite the meagre wages we received, even our small contribution was a significant addition to the family income.

I began by being the errand boy, and long and hard were the hours that I worked. Starting at eight o'clock, with one hour for lunch and half an hour for tea, I would be employed till the shop closed at six o'clock each day, except for Friday when the closing time was nine o'clock and on Saturday when the doors closed at eight-thirty. Yet these were happy days and I remember them with pleasure. Wednesday was a half day closing and so I was able to play football or tennis in the afternoon.

I worked with the Meadow Dairy for two years and progressed to being a counter hand, specialising in the provisions side of the business. Then in the autumn of 1938 I replied to an advertisement for a job in the grocery department of the local Co-op. I was delighted to be given the job and so I became a grocer's assistant and felt very grand in being part of a 'proper' grocery store.

The manager of the store was a Methodist local preacher, and on hearing that I was of the same faith and indeed very interested in its ministry he undertook to take me with him when he went to the various churches to preach. In this way I became a local preacher and having passed the appropriate examinations, decided that I would offer myself as a candidate for the Methodist ministry. I was well supported by the resident ministers and indeed spent most of my evenings after work at the Manse studying prior to seeking entry to one of the theological colleges. I was expected to preach in the many churches in the area, and often walked six miles to take morning service at one village, returned home for lunch and preached at another church in the evening. I enjoyed the experience and resolved that I would one day graduate into the Church.

Alas that was not to be. In the autumn of 1939 war was declared and immediately life-styles changed. I was just seventeen years of age and many of the young men of the town left to join the Forces. The church halls became the billets for the soldiers and the church congregations set up canteens and centres for the leisure time activities of soldiers in the town. I, too, became conscious of the possibility of my having to join the Forces. I did volunteer for the Home Guard and spent many nights patrolling the lanes looking for enemy parachutists. Many a time the air-raid sirens wailed a warning of enemy attack, but each time our town was spared. The sound of the siren sent a shiver through our spines, and, despite our uniforms, I wonder what would have happened if we had come face to face with a trained enemy parachutist. The months wore on and the outlook seemed very bleak. Following enemy bombardment from the air, the successes of the RAF during the Battle of Britain period had a stimulating effect on the morale of the people, particularly the young, and it was not long before I felt that I should offer my services to the Royal Air Force. I had learned that by volunteering one normally stood a better chance of being accepted in the branch of the Service of one's choice, and in my case this turned out to be true, because I was accepted as a trainee pilot/observer. I was taken to Padgate for my ability tests; satisfied the powers that be that I had the ability to make the grade as aircrew; was given a number and sent home to await being called up for training.

In July 1940 I was summoned to report to St John's Wood to start my life in the RAF. I will never forget that Monday morning as, accompanied by my father and younger brother, I walked down the High Street towards the railway station.

Bearing in mind that I had not been away from home before, the thought of going to London struck fear into my heart. I managed to hide my apprehension from my father, but he must have known how I felt because some twenty-five years earlier he had experienced the same moment on being called to the colours. The three-coach train drew into the station, and with all my worldly possessions in my case, I bade farewell to my father and brother and boarded the train. With a whistle and a belch of steam I was away, starting a new life in strange surroundings. I remember changing platforms at Durham station and eventually boarding an express bound for Kings Cross.

The train was packed. All seats were occupied and the corridors were packed with servicemen in uniform sitting on upturned cases I felt very inadequate and seemed not to fit into this atmosphere and it was with relief that I eventually began to converse with a young soldier who was travelling to York. The time passed very quickly and by the time my companion had reached his destination I was feeling a little more sure of myself. We parted with expressions of good luck and I was left once more to my own thoughts.

A number of people had alighted at York and I was able to find a seat in a compartment. I remember the mad scramble that ensued when the train reached Peterborough and the occupants of my compartment decided it was possible to obtain tea and a bun from one of the Forces trolleys. I joined the throng and for the first time, though not by any means the last, found myself drinking tea from a jam jar. In common with the others I returned to my seat and savoured the 'jar' of beverage, despite finding it very hot on the fingers. The jar neatly disposed of under the seat I settled down to a nap, and after several stops at stations on the way, eventually found the train entering the built up area of London. Kings Cross station was a hive of activity. Soldiers, sailors, airmen, and sundry other uniformed people hurried to and fro with heavy kit-bags or cases. Groups of servicemen were on the move with rifles slung over their shoulders and their kit piled high on the railway trolley. This then was the bewildering scene that confronted me, and I somehow had to find my way to the underground station that served St John's Wood.

I must have looked very forlorn because a young man of about my age came up to me and said that he was looking for the underground and to my relief I learned that he had been instructed, as I had, to report to the RTO at St John's Wood, and that he was starting training as air crew. We became firm friends from that day until he was killed in 1942. He was a wonderful friend and we trained together right up to the time that we were awarded our Observer Brevets at Dumfries. In this time we had spent times of leave together, either at his home or with me in Willington. He was an only son, and his mother had brought him up from his being young after his father had succumbed to injuries received in the Great War, and which necessitated his being permanently hospitalised.

On reaching our destination I was, along with several hundred more boys of a like age, taken by lorry to a block of flats in London that was to be our home during our period of training and selection. We were accommodated about five to a room in the building and it soon became apparent that everything was done at 'the double' whilst in London. This included eating our meals, which were taken in Regents Park zoo. Scarcely seated and beginning to eat we were reminded that others were outside and awaiting our departure before they could enter for their meal. We were marched around in 'flights' of fifty airmen, and everything was done at breakneck pace. Mornings began with a quick march to breakfast, and it was a race as various groups of airmen

12

converged on the zoo pavilion, only to be halted and made to wait while those who had got there earlier had their meal. Then it was our turn to enter, eat and be formed up outside for the next manoeuvre. I can honestly say that I have never been so harried in my life, and evening provided no respite. Invariably there were extra lectures or compulsory swotting periods and of course the endless periods of guard and fire picket duties. Added to this we were taken to a medical centre and given various inoculations to be followed by sessions of marching or physical training. It was to help the serum to be quickly absorbed into the system that we were subjected to arm, trunk and leg exercises. Similarly it was to our benefit to be proficient at drill, because such discipline of the body not only kept us fit but would stand us in good stead later in times of stress or danger. This we took with a pinch of salt, but it indeed was the means of saving many lives in the months that lay ahead. We were turned into a super fit outfit, responding to commands without a moment's thought and this is the essential ingredient of the professional serviceman.

The period in London had its lighter moments. As young raw recruits we were obviously at times very homesick. Letters from home meant much to us and it was with excitement that the mail was distributed each morning. Parcels too, were eagerly awaited and the arrival of these items were usually posted on sheets in the window of the 'post office', which was a ground floor room of one of the flats. My mother had told me in a letter that she was sending a parcel containing items of value and I was anxious to receive this mail as soon as possible. I therefore went to the post office to scan the list which was pasted on the window. To my surprise it was a blank sheet of paper. Suddenly a voice boomed out, "You, airman. What are you looking for?" I noticed that the owner of this voice was the Flight

Sergeant and I meekly explained that I was expecting a parcel, and since it had not been delivered with the letters I had hoped that perhaps it was in the post office. It wasn't and for my inquisitiveness the Flight Sergeant detailed me for an extra guard duty. I still had not learned my lesson and the next morning I went back to the post office to scan the paper pasted there. True enough it contained names on this occasion, but not mine. My friend the Flight Sergeant was there however, and on seeing me and remembering me from the day before, promptly detailed me for an extra fire picket duty. Enough is enough, after all, and so I resolved to await notification of the arrival of the parcel. This duly came to me when, on early morning muster parade, I was told to report to the post office to collect a parcel. Overjoyed I went at the earliest opportunity, only to be confronted by the dreaded NCO who told me in no uncertain terms that the B- - - - - parcel had been there for two days awaiting collection I was admonished for not being more prompt in collecting the parcel, and as an added punishment was awarded an extra guard duty. I went straight back to my billet and wrote home imploring my mother not to send any more parcels.

Despite these trivial incidents, and the constant bombing by the Luftwaffe, our training went ahead and we were soon considered worthy of further training. With great excitement we learned that we had been posted to No 6 ITW, Aberystwyth for the next stage of our navigational training. My friend and I were happy to know that we were both to go to Aberystwyth, and it was with a feeling of great pride that we were assembled early one morning to be taken to Paddington and thence by train to Wales. Others were being sent to different training locations, mainly in Devon. Torquay, Babbacombe, Paignton and Newquay were featured very prominently to receive would-be pilots and observers.

The journey to Aberystwyth was uneventful. We were packed like sardines into the railway coaches, but this seemed to present no hardship to any of us. We were so relieved to have passed out successfully from St John's Wood, and of course proud that we had been reclassified as Aircraftmen 1st Class, that the discomfort of being herded into a stuffy train was a minor inconvenience and one which was readily accepted. We indulged in the usual high jinks of leg pulling and hopping out at stations en route in search of the usual cup of tea and a 'wad' and eventually the train pulled into the station at Aberystwyth. The familiar sight of the canvas tilted lorries greeted us as we were assembled in the station forecourt, and with kit-bags and personal baggage we were driven to the next billet. This happened to be in the Queen's Hotel, right on the sea front, and we disembarked from the lorries and filed into the building and into the rooms that were to be our homes for the next few months. Again I was lucky in that my friend and I were able to keep together in the same room and, with the other four occupants, we selected our bed spaces.

I must say that after being in the heart of London, the view from the window of our room was idyllic. Ahead lay a stretch of beautiful sand, and this together with the breaking of the waves and the wheeling and shrieking of the seagulls presented a picture of absolute heaven. This picture was soon to be changed a little as we assembled in PT kit outside the hotel and on the sea front which had earlier filled us with such delight. Drill and PT was always performed on the sea front, and invariably we had an audience of the local townspeople who were amused at some of the misfortunes that can befall a human being who is self-conscious about parading in public. It is not easy to be nonchalant when falling flat on one's face doing leap frog, or turning to the right when the order, clearly given, was for turning to the left. I must say that for the first few weeks at Aberystwyth most of us felt a little hostile towards the spectators who always seemed to turn up at the most inconvenient time. I well remember on one occasion that I would willingly have liked the ground to open up and swallow me from the gaze of the public. We were in PT kit being put through our paces on the roadway outside the Queen's Hotel where we were billeted. We were 'playing' at horseback fighting. This meant that one of the trainees acted as horse and had another on his back as rider. The object of the exercise was to pull at another rider till he was forced to dismount. Often however a heavy fall ensued and this was no laughing matter since it was uncomfortable, to say the least, to be thrown onto the road after losing one's balance. On the first 'joust' my jockey was a lad of four foot nothing, and weight to match. I was a six foot nothing fellow and whilst not a 'bruiser' in build was very capable of carrying my rider. Things altered however when the instructor called "change over". Now I was a six foot jockey on a four foot horse, and inevitably I hit the ground with a resounding thump. To make matters worse the whole of the population of Aberystwyth seemed to have turned out to witness my 'downfall', and it was a relief when I was helped into the hotel to await transportation to the local hospital to have my scrapes and bruises dealt with.

However, we soon became hardened to the routine and in a short time were able to accept the public gaze quite philosophically, and as we became more proficient at PT and drill we became even proud to be showing our new found talent for obeying commands without hesitation. We began to enjoy the physical aspect of our training and looked forward to our long cross country runs up Constitutional Hill, and our football matches against other units, sometimes from the Army. In addition we were marched to and from our lectures at a pace that was frightening to behold. The best Infantry Regiment had nothing on the ITW recruit when it came to marching pace. There was little wonder that the physical training and the mental studying left us at the end of the day welcoming the barrack bed and lights out. Those of you who might think that such effort was rather harsh can be forgiven for such thoughts, but there was more.

There were additional duties to be performed on a rota basis. Every night sentries were posted outside our billets, and we performed this duty as a four hour stint. Armed with a rifle we marched a measured beat, halted, turned about and then marched back. We were to challenge anyone approaching the billet, although heaven knows what would have happened if our challenge had been answered by a foreign accent. Fire picket was also one of the hated 'chores'. This entailed being at a state of readiness in case the siren was sounded to warn of an air-raid. In the time that I was at Aberystwyth I do not recall any air-raid, but I do remember the times when the warning was sounded. It seemed incredible but the siren always seemed to wail about 2 a.m., and as the heavens were opening to disgorge their surfeit of water. On one occasion I was on duty when the warning went. It was about 2 a.m. and the rain was like stair rods. The vantage point for the fire picket was on the roof of the hotel. There was a small square flat area, surrounded by a metal railing, very similar to the type one sees in very old cemeteries surrounding tombs. The access to this platform was via a wooden ladder in the roof, and on hearing the siren I was duly dispatched to my post, midway between heaven and earth. I do not remember when I have ever spent such an uncomfortable night in this country. The rain lashed down, the waves broke with a roar on the beach and in the inky blackness nothing else stirred. I came to the conclusion that

17

had there been a raid that night, the town would have come to no harm from incendiary bombing. When the 'all clear' was sounded I descended, like a drowned rat, to the fire picket room, happy in the knowledge that, while the inhabitants of Aberystwyth slept, I had mounted vigil to keep them safe. I was rewarded with one of the worst colds that I have ever had, and because of forced absences from lectures had to work doubly hard on my recovery to keep up with the rest of the course, and not be faced with re-coursing, which was the dread of every aspiring aviator.

There were of course the lighter moments in our stay at the Queen's Hotel. We were well looked after by the townspeople, who invited us to their homes. I attended the local Methodist Church and was adopted by a very nice family, living in Edgehill Road. I was always welcomed by Mr and Mrs Edwards and family, and I owe a great debt to them for the kindness they showed me whilst I was in Aberystwyth. There, too, were cinema shows, and of course one could never forget the 'variety' shows put on in the Kings Hall by ourselves and other amateurs. One highlight of our stay was when a floating mine was washed against the pier supports and demolished the cinema at the end of that structure. I think I am right in saying it was a cinema, although the passage of time makes this fact somewhat doubtful. In any event it was a hall of some description.

We had arrived to start our training in Wales on Sunday the 3rd of August, 1941. The date sticks in my memory because it is the birthday of one of my sisters. Our training was now completed at the initial stage. We had been schooled in subjects such as navigation, signals, meteorology, principles of flight, aircraft recognition signals, etc., and we were now ready to move on to the next stage in our flying career. We left Aberystwyth at 6.10 p.m. on 15th November, and our next unit was to be in Scotland, at the Air Observer School, Dumfries, at which station we arrived on Saturday the 16th at 10.30 a.m. On reflection it is incredible to recall that most moves within the Forces begin very early – whilst most normal folk are still in bed – or very late – when most normal folk are going to bed. There is nothing like being in a railway carriage compartment, with the blinds drawn, thus excluding any chance of fresh air, and so succumbing to the fug created by the twelve inhabitants, half of whom smoked incessantly. Such was our journey up to, and over, the border. In addition to our going up in the world, in terms of latitude, we had been promoted to the exalted rank of Leading Aircraftmen and this promotion meant that we were to receive three shillings and sixpence a day instead of the two shillings and sixpence we had been paid hitherto. That extra one shilling a day meant a great deal to most of us, because it meant we could increase the voluntary allotment that we were making to our families.

We arrived at Dumfries at 10.30 a.m. and were greeted by the sight of the lorries with the canvas tilts, which were the usual means of transporting groups of men from railway station to their new unit. Come to think of it, such transport was often used to transport aircrews from mess to their aircraft just before a raid. One had to be fairly fit to be able to clamber aboard, and then there was always the added burden of kit-bag, case, tin hat and gas-mask to contend with. We had arrived at Number 10, AOS ready for our next period of training which was to include flying on practical navigation exercises, the dropping of dummy bombs and the firing at targets being towed by other aircraft. The duties of the Air Observer also involved the taking of photographs and making reports on any item of military importance that was taking place below. The course was intensive; the subjects many and varied, and the pressure put upon us by the thought of possible failure was very real. Add to this the discomfort experienced by the first flights and the reader will perhaps sense what a harrowing time was ahead of us as we disembarked from the transport on that morning in November 1941. What lay ahead was unknown but we were spurred on by our instructors who had themselves been in our position some months before, but who had in the meantime become veterans having earned a well deserved rest from a tour of operations over enemy territory. We had hitherto been divorced from the 'real' Air Force, having spent most of our time in classrooms or on the drill square.

I recall that there were twenty of us, split into two flights, and given the labels 'C' and 'D' squads. I was allocated to 'D' squad, together with my friend Dennis, and since our flying training was normally done in pairs, we were able to continue the close friendship we had forged since meeting on Kings Cross station. Excitement mounted and we felt very important as we received our flying kit. A helmet, warm leather gauntlet gloves, a warm one piece flying suit and fur lined calf length boots made us feel that at last we were ready to take on the Luftwaffe. However we were to find that the next few weeks were to be some of the most hectic so far.

The working hours usually began with our rising at 7.30 a.m. each day, except Saturday which was to be, normally, our day 'off'. Breakfast was at 8 a.m. and we then went to our classroom in time for 8.30 a.m. Lessons were conducted till 12.30 at which time we went for lunch, to return to the classroom for 1.30 p.m. start to the afternoon lessons which finished at 5 p.m. when we were free to go to tea and then to our billets. Unless we were detailed for guard or fire picket duties we were not required for duty until the next morning, but most of us went back to the classroom for private study after our 7 p.m. supper. It was most difficult to try to study in our billet which accommodated twenty-five airmen. The huts were heated by two coke stoves, one at either end, and it was amazing to what use the heaters were put. Despite this however, one night each week was a domestic night, and the occupants of each billet were required to prepare the room for inspection the next morning. This meant that each bed space lino was carefully waxed with mansion polish and then with the aid of a 'bumper', was polished until the surface fairly glistened. Woe betide any bedspace that failed to pass the scrutiny of the officer inspecting the building. This invariably meant that the whole hut was penalised and ordered to prepare for an inspection on another day, and often those whose bedspace was not up to standard were given extra duties or fatigues. I suppose that all of us who were subjected to 'bull' nights can smile as we look back on those chores, but at the time they were very irksome and a source of lowering of morale.

Our flying started at 11.45 on the 23rd November. In a De Havilland Rapide, or Dominie. Five of us flew from base, Moffat, Gretna Green, Carlisle, Penrith, Wigton, Maryport, Workington, Dalbeatie back to base on an air experience and map reading exercise. It was, for us all, a milestone in our young lives. The Dominie was a biplane and very slow. I remember we flew at about 2,000 feet at an average air speed of 120 mph. Most of us felt uncomfortable on this first flight, and although only one of us had to resort to the 'paper bag', most of us were relieved to have come through the baptism without being air sick. We did several more similar flights designed to acclimatise us to being in the air and to read the map. This was the cause of our feeling uncomfortable. It is not easy to scan a map and then to look down to identify features on the ground, well knowing that the pilot might call for a pin-point and we were all anxious to be found competent. I recall that we made one or two flights with the aircraft windows tinted to simulate night flying conditions.

Our training continued with classroom lectures covering subjects such as morse, instruction on the construction and function of aircraft instruments such as the compass, the altimeter, air speed indicator, hand held camera and bomb sight. The prime subjects were maps and charts, dead reckoning navigation, meteorology and astro navigation. Add to this some many hours of PT and drill, not forgetting the cross country runs and organised games and the reader will get an idea of how very full our days were, and how very fit we must have been to have withstood the added pressure of being away from home and always conscious of failing some test and being recoursed or, worse still, remustered because of unsuitability. There was of course a lighter side of life. Practically each week we were able to go to the ENSA concert on the camp for which we paid the princely sum of 3d to see a show that varied from the sublime to the ridiculous. Then of course we had weekly forays into Dumfries, and spent a day shopping and visiting the various cafés and going to the cinema before we dashed to catch the last bus to camp, a distance of some four miles from the town.

Soon our flying exercises began to take on a more advanced role. Having completed our familiarisation and map reading exercise, we were paired off to start our navigation flights. Dennis and I were able to pair together, and on one flight he would be 1st Navigator whilst I did the map reading, photography or reconnaissance of the terrain over which we were flying. The roles were reversed for the next flight and so we began to put into practice some of the theory of the classroom. Bombing theory had been part of our classroom lessons and we now progressed to flights in our second type of aircraft, the Fairey Battle. Solidly built monoplanes and powered by a single engine, the Battle was slow and very cumbersome from the pupils point of view. The pilots of the Battle flight were all Polish, and since, in the air, conversation between pilot and crew was by means of a piece of rubber piping, this combined with the strong accent of some of the pilots made communication difficult.

The aircraft would be parked outside the dispersal hut cum classroom, and the trainees were expected to be aboard before the pilot. Our bombing position was in the belly of the aircraft, underneath the pilot's cockpit. The master-switches for the bombs were in the cockpit, and it was part of the patter for the trainee to say, "Bombs selected" which would bring the reply from the pilot, "Number one bomb selected". Having used the bomb sight to determine the right moment to press the bomb release, the trainee would say, "Number one bomb gone". The settings we used for the bomb sight such as the speed and height of the aircraft were given by the pilot, while the wind speed and direction was either given to us at base or we had to determine it by various means on the way to the target area just off Little Ross in the Solway Firth. We had high level, low level and application exercises, the results of which were collated to arrive at the final assessment of our capabilities as bomb aimers. It is a well known saying that bad workmen blame their tools, but it is equally felt, at least among our course students, that bomb aimers blame their pilots. Guiding the pilot to the target by giving instructions such as 'left-left', intoned slowly, or 'right' spoken more quickly was never easy, and when it came to 'steady – steady' the damned pilot had never heard of the word. In any case the Battle was never an ideal aircraft for the dropping of bombs. I shall never forget one flight to the target. I have just mentioned that the bomb switches were located in the cockpit and were in the control of the pilot. Unless he put down the switches, no bomb could be released. It was common practice for the trainee to select an imaginary target, such as a farmhouse, whilst on the way to the target, and to press the bomb button at what was adjudged to be the right moment. On this occasion I was guilty of such fanciful practice, and at the precise moment when target and bomb-sight cursor was in line, I pressed the bomb button. Imagine my horror when I saw hurtling down to earth, toward what had been an imaginary target, three eleven pound practice bombs. With a scream of terror I yelled to the pilot, and sensed by his action that he was not amused. He must have inadvertently caught the switches as he got into the cockpit thus making the bombs 'live'. It was lucky for all concerned that my aim was very poor, and the bombs landed harmlessly in open fields, but of course some irate farmer was quickly on the phone to the Adjutant, and as a result the practice of bombing targets on the way to the range ceased.

On arrival at Dumfries we had been told that we faced several months of intensive work, and that we were not to rely on leave. Christmas drew nearer and with it the talk of leave. This proved to be wishful thinking and we were told officially that we would in all probability be granted three or four days leave in the New Year. Despite the disappoint-ment we were very grateful for the way in which all the service and voluntary helpers organised concerts, parties and a splendid Christmas dinner. Our families played their part in trying to make our Christmas enjoyable, and despite the stringent rationing many parcels were received from home full of 'goodies' which meant that those who had packed them had denied themselves in order to compensate us for not being at home. Indeed the billet was quite festive with decorations and cards festooned from the ceiling, and needless to say the NAAFI, Airmen's Club and the mess were suitably decorated. The menu for Christmas dinner is

The author photographed shortly after passing out
of training and having been awarded his Air Observer
Brevet and Sergeant Stripes.

Short Stirling of 'XV' Flight Alconbury. Delivered for service in August 1941, 'T' Tommy was a write-off from battle damage having reached home base after a raid on Nuremberg, two months later.

Sergeant Observer Dennis John Rushton, whom the
author refers to as having met on arrival in London
to join his first unit. They became inseparable friends
and were together for the whole of their training until
they were each crewed up.
They went to Number 218 Squadron together, but
the author was posted to Number 214 Squadron for a
tour of operations. Sadly Dennis was lost while returning
from a raid over Dusseldorf at the beginning of
September 1942.

The author stands beside an Avro Anson before setting off on a routine training exercise. Taken in the winter of 1941, at No 10 Air Observer School, Dumfries.

AIRMEN'S CLUB

Xmas Dinner Party

At 19.00 on Christmas Eve,

24th December, 1941.

Dinner at the Airmens' Club, 10 AOS, Dumfries cost sixpence and this included entertainment. The following day, Thursday — Christmas day, the menu in the Airmens' mess was: Soup, fish, turkey, ham, sausages, three vegetables and Christmas pudding, washed down by a ration of beer. The evening ENSA concert cost 3d each.

Two crews relax outside their accommodation at 1651 HCU Waterbeach in June 1942, while on a conversion course from Wellington bombers to four engined Stirlings.

Pupils of Number 10 AOS Dumfries – November 1941.

Left to right. Standing: P. Walker, P.W. Moffatt, C.A. Anderson, R. Turner, J.W.C. Clark, C. Penna, D.J. Rushton, A. Alexander, T.C. Robinson, J.F. Perry. Sitting: E. Walton, E. Tingley, R.M. Boyle, E. Williams, R.L. Double, F.S.K. Watt, J.L. Kemp, J. Sahler, L.M. Jones, J. Martin.

Dusseldorf
—100,000
fire-bombs

MORE than 100,000 incendiary bombs were dropped on Dusseldorf in Thursday night's RAF raid, the heaviest yet on a moonless night.

Flares and the fires did the moon's job. Before long Dusseldorf was a furnace.

Streets, buildings and the Rhine were lit up for the following aircraft carrying high-explosive bombs.

The whole attack took just under an hour. Indications are that damage was on a vast scale.

Several hundred b o m b e r s made the attack on Dusseldorf and other west German targets, while fighter aircraft patrolled enemy-occupied territory. Thirty-one of our aircraft are missing. The fighters destroyed one enemy plane.

Author's first raid.

Two USAF aircrew with resistance members in South of France.

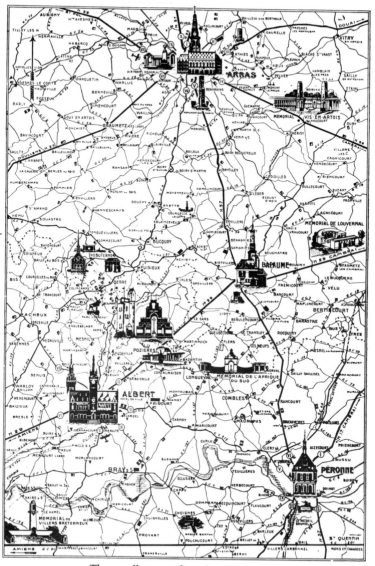

The small map referred to on page 47.

worth a mention, and I have it on record that we had soup, fish, turkey, ham, sausage and stuffing, three vegetables and Christmas pudding. Beer was served to all who wanted it and the 'waiters' were the officers and senior NCO's of the permanent staff.

We began 1942 by having the promised break between the 3rd and 5th of January, both days inclusive. This was to be our first visit home since arriving at Dumfries, and we were all anxious to get home to see our families, relax and doubtless indulge in a little harmless 'line-shooting'. The break was soon over and we were back to our training schedule on the morning of the 6th January. Indeed at 9.50 a.m. Dennis and I were in the air flying a navigational exercise, a flight which lasted for two hours, the route being base, Kirkoswald, Moffatt, Glenluce and back to base. There was now another distraction. We had heard from reliable sources that we might be posted abroad to complete our flying training. Many and varied were the exotic places mentioned but such rumour was quickly scotched and we settled down to our routine work.

We were now spending more time in the classroom because of severe weather conditions making flying impossible. Low cloud, sleet, snow and extreme cold meant cancellation of flying detail day after day. Indeed on the night of Saturday/Sunday the 17th/18th of January, so heavy was the fall of snow that all personnel were engaged all night in snow clearance on the runway to keep the airfield open. It was a daunting, hopeless task and in the end the elements won. More snow fell and we were not able to make any headway. Our flying programme was not resumed until early February, and to break the monotony we were granted a period of leave from the 7th to the 10th. The weather improved considerably from this point to enable us to fly most days, and our types of aircraft flown was increased by our exercises in the Blackburn Botha, an aircraft that had not too good a name for serviceability or performance. We were to conduct our firing exercises in these aircraft, and to do this we were required to get into the mid-upper turret. I was in great difficulty here, since I was six foot tall and there was precious little room in the turret once I had struggled into it. I recall that we flew over the sea doing air to ground firing and on occasions we were joined by another aircraft towing a drogue — a sausage-like banner attached by a long line to its tail — and it was our task to fire at the drogue and the number of 'hits' was the measure of our competence. I am sure that the pilot of the towing aircraft must have had nine lives, because I expect that some of our misses on the drogue must have been very nearly 'hits' on the tail of his aircraft. Meanwhile in our aircraft the spent cartridge cases were ejected all around our feet in the turret, thus adding to the discomfort already described.

We were pleased to see the back of February 1942, because in the whole month we had only been able to fly on six occasions with a total flying time of eleven hours. True there had been the lighter moments when we had, several of us, met in Binns Café in Dumfries and had tea followed by a shopping expedition in the town. Dennis purchased a second-hand gramophone and, since Glenn Miller was all the rage, we bought some of his records to play in our recreational hours in the billet. That evening we decided en bloc to go to the Lyceum Cinema to see Leslie Banks and Alistair Sim in *Cottage to Let*. Having taken over one whole row of seating we decided that the music being played before the film began was not as good as that on the records we had just purchased. We had the gramophone and the records so we decided to play Glenn Miller. Naturally this did not amuse the management or the other patrons and we were very quickly put in our place by a threat that the

Commanding Officer would be told of our behaviour if we continued to cause a nuisance. This had the desired effect of putting the necessary damper on our high spirits, and we settled down to watch what I remember was a very good English film. That gramophone did sterling service in billet and classroom and did much to brighten our off duty moments, as well as earning us camp fatigues on a couple of occasions when we played music when we should have been studying.

Very soon we were advanced far enough in our studies to be able to undertake more difficult and lengthy exercise, usually in the Botha but we now were flying in one of the wars favourite aircraft, the Avro Anson. After the Dominie, Battle and Botha we all felt that this aircraft was the Rolls-Royce of aircraft. We did navigation exercises, air reconnaissance trips and photography and very often ended the flight by dropping bombs on the range, which added a touch of realism, excitement and pride. We felt that at last we were doing things right. To be able to fly a circuitous route, find a target and bomb it with a fair degree of accuracy seemed to be very near the real thing. In addition our navigation log work, photography and reconnaissance reports kept us so busy that we had little time to waste, and it seemed no time from taking off to landing even though two or three hours had elapsed. Always Dennis and I flew together and this was a source of joy to us both since we had forged such a link of friendship that it was second nature to help each other in times of difficulty. This team spirit, started in training, was to prove invaluable later when we were to part and form part of a crew of a bomber, flying in raids over enemy territory.

March, April and May in 1942 was a period of reasonable weather, and this being so our training was not very much interrupted. We did a lot of flying and in between we had the usual lectures and of course progress tests. We all seemed to be getting satisfactory results and the course instructors were well satisfied with our progress and were confident that we would pass the final examinations and qualify for our Observer brevets. This confidence was not misplaced because on Sunday 17th May we officially passed out of training, were given our brevet and promoted to the rank of Sergeant. We also had been given our postings to our next unit, which was to be an Operational Training Unit, at which we would be crewed up with a pilot, wireless operator and air-gunners. Dennis and I were still in luck since we were posted to an OTU in Scotland, namely Lossiemouth on the Moray Firth.

It is difficult to describe the feeling of pride, mixed with a little relief, which we had as we were paraded and each presented with our brevet and stripes. That evening needles and cotton did overtime as we struggled to sew these treasures to our uniform. On the 10th July 1941 we had been raw recruits but now on the 17th May 1942 we had reached the end of our classroom training and were to embark on what was to be the most important part of our flying career. Life from now on was to assume a more serious aspect and the aircraft and fellow aircrew were to be those that were capable of being sent on sorties against the enemy.

We were posted to Lossiemouth and arrived at that station on Tuesday 19th May, and were greeted with the news that we were to be crewed up as bomb aimers, which classification had been introduced because of the four engined bombers coming into commission. However, whilst at Lossiemouth, we would be crewed up to man the Wellington bombers which were to be our next aircraft. This being so we met our pilot, and other members of our crew, and from that time on we were to be a team. I was crewed with a New Zealand pilot, a wireless operator from Manchester, a rear gunner from Cardiff, all of us being Sergeants, and an officer from

London. The five of us were to fly as a crew, working as a team, and eventually would be posted to a squadron for operational duties.

Some two months elapsed during which time we had flown on daylight and night exercises and on the 24th July, after a brief period of leave we reported to number 214 Squadron, Stradishall, in Suffolk. We were told that we were to fly the new Stirling four engined bomber, and have our crew increased by the addition of a flight engineer and a mid-upper gunner. This transition would entail a conversion course at a nearby Conversion Unit, and so we were sent to 1651 Conversion Unit, Waterbeach, and met our two new crew members, both Sergeants.

Now, as a crew of seven, we were introduced to the four engined Stirling and for the next four weeks we flew day and night, weather permitting, to acclimatise ourselves to the aircraft and to get to know the new members of the crew. Having become very much attached to the Wellington, it was indeed quite daunting to fly in the biggest aeroplane in service at the time. A great deal of skill was necessary to take off and land the aircraft, which when the wheels were down stood twenty-two feet from the ground. The undercarriage was so delicate that any 'cross' landing invariably meant that the aircraft would come to an ignominious ending on its 'belly'. Fortunately Frank, our pilot, was a very capable airman, and in a very short time he had mastered the intricacies of the Stirling and proved to be an exceptional pilot.

Life at Waterbeach was very pleasant, and when we had time off from flying we visited Ely and the neighbouring towns. I can well remember a daily occurrence to which we all looked forward. When flying in the afternoon we usually had time to sit on the grass outside the aircraft, which was parked in the dispersal circle by the side of the road that ran from Waterbeach to Ely. We soon made friends with the driver of a bakery van that used the route to Ely each day, and inevitably it became a habit for the van to stop and watch the preparations for the aircraft to take off. An introductory wave was followed by conversation, and from then on we always had a bag of buns and cakes to enjoy when our flying ceased for the day. I often think of that van and the kindness of the driver, and no doubt the custom would continue after we had gone, and the new crew to occupy that dispersal point would be treated in a similar fashion.

Our last flight from Waterbeach was on the 5th September, and on the 8th September we flew our Stirling, R9350, to the 214 Squadron airfield, Stradishall. We were very elated because we were now among operational crews and knew that we would be detailed for raids over enemy territory almost at once. Despite this feeling of apprehension and excitement I secretly had sadness in that Dennis had remained at 218 Squadron, Marham, and for the first time we were parted. I was to see him only once again before he was killed returning from a raid over Germany.

On the 10th September we took off to bomb Dusseldorf. With mixed feelings we arrived at the aircraft in the crew bus. We were excited, apprehensive but carried along on the wave of enthusiasm that seemed to exude from the more experienced crews round about. We took off at 21.20 and I will always remember the green light that flashed to give Frank permission to start his take off run. I was in the 2nd pilot's seat to assist take off, and I also recall the pride that we felt as we moved forward and saw the wave from the CO and several others who were always at take off to wish the crews god speed. We were soon airborne, and with our load of incendiaries we made from Cromer, and then set course for our target. There was no idle chatter over the intercom now. Silence was golden and was only to be broken when any member had some urgent report to make. The front, mid-upper and rear turrets were now the eyes of the aircraft, and a vigilant watch was kept for marauding enemy aircraft about which we had heard much from those well versed in operational flying. We saw several other bombers on the way to the target but as luck would have it, no enemy fighters.

It was not long before we saw ahead a virtual cauldron of fire and light. The pathfinders had illuminated the target and earlier aircraft had dropped their bombs and the glare from the ground, coupled with the numerous searchlights and streams of tracer bullets and flashes from exploding anti-aircraft gun shells, mesmerised us all. It was the first sight of action and the enormity of it killed any sense of fear. We were approaching the target and ready to make our bombing run. I was lying on my stomach gazing down on all the action below, feeling very elated. Somewhere below there was a factory that we had to hit and put out of action. I had set the height, speed and wind direction on the bomb site, had muttered "bomb doors open" when a cone of searchlight hit me full in the face and the aircraft seemed to be 'frying'. The heat seemed to be intense and the natural reaction was to get out of it as fast as possible. This we did. The pilot banked sharply to port and away from the inferno.

This was not the answer however, and we soon realised that we had to go through the 'flak' and searchlights, drop our load and get off home. Again we turned into the target, only to be coned again, and evasive action took us away from the area. We were now all at sea and confused. Frank now took control and said we were going in. This we did and I was amazed how coolly I followed the target along the bomb sight, and at the precise moment pressed the bomb release. This sent hundreds of small incendiary bombs on their way to the ground: activated the switch that sent down the flare from the rear of the aircraft and started the camera in motion to photograph the point of contact of our bombs. With our load discharged we turned for the safety of the comparative darkness outside the target area, but we were again coned. This time we could not escape, and it seemed that, despite the evasive action taken, the searchlight crew were intent on keeping us in their sights. Eventually, and to our intense relief, we were in darkness again, and it was a time to reflect on what had happened. Quietness reigned again, and I know that we all thought of the crews that had not been so lucky and had not survived. We saw several aircraft in flames, and noted one or two parachutes silhouetted against the fires on the ground. One could only surmise that, with the shells exploding all around them, they had a very poor chance of reaching the ground safely.

We landed back at base at 1.30 a.m., clambered into our crew bus and were driven back for debriefing. Even then the enormity of the happenings of the past few hours had not been realised by us. The more experienced crews reported that the enemy defences were very strong and said that they had had one of their most difficult operations. We had no other trips to judge the truth of this, but all felt that if things were no worse in the future then we would survive. It appears that some four hundred and seventy-nine aircraft were used on this raid and thirty-three aircraft were lost. There was much damage done to Dusseldorf and the surrounding area, and fifty-two firms were obliged to cease production for various periods of time. Many houses had been damaged and many people were killed or injured. We were not to know of this at the time, and so the results of our bombing seemed to be so remote that we were not aware of the carnage, damage and suffering we must have caused. We were aware however of the number of airmen who had been lost, and it was very personal when I learned that Dennis had been one of the casualties. His aircraft had ditched in the sea off the Dutch coast, and though some of his crew had been able to get into their dinghy, and were picked up by rescue boats, no trace was ever found of him and he went down with the aircraft.

We returned to our quarters after a meal, weary but thankful that we had survived our baptism of fire. The night had been too eventful for us to fully comprehend what we had been through. Sleep did not come, however, and one by one we realised that the older hands had been right in their assessment of the situation, and that our inexperience had possibly played a great part in our survival, and I can say that future operations were always approached with more caution and trepidation.

Other targets quickly followed of which Essen and Hamburg were the most heavily defended. Kiel, too, was quite a hot spot, since the late comers were fired on, not only by the static defences, but by the warships that were in the base but that had hitherto not announced their presence until the raid was well and truly under way. What was most noticeable was the contrast of the searchlight batteries in England and Germany. It must be said that our searchlights were as candle in comparison, and the numbers and their intensity had to be seen to be believed. It was a common occurrence for an aircraft to be handed from one cone to another, and to be so held for a considerable time despite evasive action. This was extremely disconcerting and dangerous, because the fighter aircraft were invariably lurking around and attacking those unfortunate enough to be pin-pointed.

The bomber offensive was now gathering momentum, and various moves were afoot to increase the number of conversion units, and on the 1st October 1942 Stradishall became the base for the newly formed 1657 Conversion Unit. This meant that 214 Squadron had to move to a satellite aerodrome at Chedburgh, some ten miles north east of Stradishall, and on the A143 towards Bury St Edmunds. We were very sad at leaving Stradishall because it was a pre-war station and the accommodation and amenities were first class. It had opened in February 1938, and became the 'home' of number 214 Squadron from February 1940. Many raids had been mounted in that time and of course many losses had been incurred. It was with mixed feelings that we took off at 14.10 on Thursday, 1st October and flew the short distance, a mere forty minutes flying time from take off to landing, to what was to be our new airfield. Chedburgh had opened on the 7th September and was to be the base for 214 Squadron until late in 1943. We were not enamoured with our new surroundings. After leaving such sumptuous accommodation Chedburgh provided a very spartan alternative. As I recollect, mud was everywhere and it was imperative to keep to the concrete paths while moving from building to building. We had little time to indulge in self pity because of the task of settling in and local flying to get used to the new approach and landing features of the airfield. On the 6th October we were detailed for the first raid from our new station. On that night we took off at 19.27 for Osnabruck, and after a fairly uneventful trip landed back at around midnight. A couple of mine laying trips followed in quick succession, one of which was to the Baltic Sea and which was undertaken by a small force with relatively few casualties.

Towards the end of October the targets chosen were in Italy. This strategy coincided with the successes the armies were having in Africa, and so the attention of Bomber Command was turned to the cities of Italy, one could only surmise as a 'softening up' preparation before an assault by land was made. Our first target was Genoa. On the 23rd October we set off at 18.45 on the long haul over France, the

Alps and into Italy. A force of 122 aircraft was employed and the flight across France was uneventful. There was good cloud cover but the experience of crossing the Alps was rather daunting. There were times when it appeared that the aircraft would never clear the next peak, and I am sure that this fact, together with the extreme cold accounted for some of the losses we sustained in attacking Italian targets. Having reached Genoa we found that the city was covered with cloud, which cover extended over the sea. We decided to go down low to try to pierce the cloud base, and so we approached the city from the sea. Lying on my stomach in the customary bombing position I suddenly saw looming up ahead a tall obelisk, perhaps a lighthouse. I was sure that we would hit it but with great dexterity Frank tipped the wing and just avoided it. The violent movement of the aircraft was not appreciated by those of the crew who had not seen the obstruction, but this was yet another occasion when we had just cause to be grateful for the skill and courage of Frank. We swung to the starboard and at a height of about three hundred feet we flashed over the marshalling yards of Genoa. We were assisted in our identification of the target by searchlights, situated on the hills surrounding the city, who tried to pick us up and in doing so lit up the terrain below. Our bombs were released and with parting shots from the mid-upper and rear turrets we turned out into the cloud again. It was all over in seconds, and exhilarating it was to flash over the ground at such a low altitude. I may say we never did it again, on the advice of those at base who had the planning and organisational responsibility. The aircraft received several hits from light gunfire and we had to land at Duxford on our return, being short of fuel and in difficulties. We were able to take off again, next day, and after fifteen minutes flying landed at base.

Luck had been on our side up till now, and apart from

being peppered by fragments of shells and coming home with numerous holes of various sizes in the aircraft's fuselage, no great trauma was experienced. On one of these raids Gerry, our mid-upper gunner had received a piece of shrapnel in the back of his head, but we were able to get him back safely and he recovered fully after a spell in the sick bay. November had been a very quiet month for the Squadron, and mine laying trips had been the main activity. On the 28th November we were detailed for another raid on Turin, this time to attack the Fiat motor works. We were told that it would be mounted by only a few aircraft, and as take off time approached we were concerned about the weather conditions at base. We had been warned that the weather forecast was bad, and that the route over the Alps could be fraught with icing conditions. We took off at 18.30 and steadily climbed to six thousand feet and set course for Italy. The journey to the target was indeed uneventful and we met little opposition. The weather it seemed was too bad for much flying. We did experience bad conditions over the Alps, but having negotiated this obstacle nothing stood between us and the target. The pathfinders had done their job and, having pin-pointed the target we ran in at about fifteen hundred feet. We tried another run because our first was well off line and because of the height we had little time to correct our error. At the second attempt we were able to discharge our load, and we began the slow climb back towards the Alps and home. We found this period of climb quite worrying because we were sitting targets if attacked by fighters. We were struggling to gain height and therefore sacrificed speed. Nevertheless we were success-ful and eventually reached the comparative safety of France and, in our opinion, we had surmounted the worst obstacle.

We were all feeling very cold and uncomfortable. These flights into Italy from UK certainly taxed the stamina of the crews. On this occasion we were more than usually concerned because we had taken as our rear gunner and mid-upper gunner two new members with whom we had not flown before, and to my recollection were making their first trip to Italy. I think that most crews were rather superstitious about a change of personnel, and I have often thought how much worse it must have been for the new members who were also flying for the first time with a new crew. Silence was, as usual, observed and apart from a few shells being fired from the ground we were lulled into a false sense of security by the lack of enemy opposition. We were just north of Paris, the time around midnight when the whole aircraft shuddered. A loud bang and instantly we were enveloped by tracer bullets. I heard a scream over the intercom and instantly went to the second pilots seat in case the skipper had been the one to need help. I found him quite unhurt but struggling valliantly to take evasive action. The controls were limp and still the shells were being pumped into us. He gave the abandon aircraft order, and we acted on those instructions. Fire had now broken out in the aircraft, and before leaving his seat Frank opened the throttles to try to keep the aircraft aloft as long as possible to allow us to get out.

I clipped my parachute to my harness, and tumbled into the inky blackness from the forward escape hatch, closely followed by two other members of the crew. I found myself suspended in air with nothing but the silken cords of my parachute to see me down safely. I saw two other parachutes, but soon became engrossed in looking below to see what my landing area would be. The aircraft had by this time disappeared and suddenly the sky was lit up as it crashed some distance away, and all was quiet except for the wind rushing past my ears. I was able to see quite clearly that I was going to land in some water. I had looked down and in the moonlight had seen what I thought were waves. This did worry me because I was no swimmer and it was bitterly cold. Had I been in command of my senses I would have realised that I couldn't be over the sea, and that whatever I was seeing below was therefore not water. Indeed I nearly did panic and inflate my mae west, but thought better of it since it might have been damaged by the webbing of my parachute. I was so busy with these thoughts that I was totally unprepared for the sudden landing. However on reflection I concluded that it was a good thing because I hit the ground completely relaxed and escaped injury. True I was winded for a while, but above all I was very bemused and uncertain as to what lay ahead.

The mystery of the waves was now unfolded. The field in which I had landed had recently been ploughed, and the moonlight was glistening on the wet earth ridges, and so from above it would take on the form of troughs and waves. I saw nearby a pile of what looked to be turnips but turned out to be sugar beet. My head was now clearing and I instinctively pulled in the white canopy of my chute, rolled it into some kind of ball, and this, together with my harness, I stuffed into one of the piles of beet and covered over all traces. I could still hear the drone overhead, of aircraft going home and this momentarily added to the feeling of helplessness that came over me. It was bitterly cold, dark and damp. I had not been sitting long when from the distance an engine came along its line and a very bright searchlight began to play over the fields in my direction. I still had on my flying helmet, Irving jacket and trousers and my calf length leather flying boots. I had the presence of mind to lie flat on my face and I can only assume, if the light did ever reach me, that my brown attire blended in with the surrounding terrain. Soon the sound of the engine receded into the distance, and I was once again left to myself in the stillness of the night.

Remembering the content of some of my earlier lectures, I realised that it was imperative that I moved immediately, and that the direction of my escape must be away from the scene of the aircraft crash. It was natural that the enemy would throw a cordon around the area, and search inwards, especially as the parachutes must have been seen and it was obvious that some of us at least had reached the ground and were at large. Moving away from the aircraft meant that the distance between the searchers would be greater, and there was a better chance of slipping through the net. I hurriedly put my Mae West under another pile of beet and started to run. It was now that I began to bless the many hours of drill and PT that we had been subjected to in our training. Even so running over fields, stumbling into and across ditches was very exhausting. I was also feeling very tired and hungry, and I was getting quite frightened as I crashed along. Every small tree that lay ahead seemed to be a German soldier with his rifle at the ready. Down I would go until I overcame this dread and decided that it was safe to move. I would no longer go over fences but sought a way under, or through, attempting to keep a low profile. The moon was now covered by cloud, and though this was in some ways a blessing, I felt as if I had lost a friend.

I must have been running for three or four hours, I was still out in the country, and although I had crossed two minor roads I was careful to avoid going near to any building. I eventually decided that enough was enough and so I sought a place to have a short rest. I still was aware of the necessity for concealment, and I came into a field planted with some type of cabbage. I lay between the rows, pulled up some of the green vegetable and covered myself and fell into a fitful sleep. I say fitful, because I was so cold and hungry that I kept waking and certainly not relishing my bed. I could only have lain there for a matter of an hour or so, and when I awoke for the last time I saw that it was getting very light. I took stock of my position and saw that I was in a field that ran alongside a road, or vice versa since to me at the time I was very disorientated. On the other side of the road I saw a group of farm buildings and I resolved to dash across the road into one of those buildings and see what happened. I must have cut a funny sight as I trundled over the road. My flying suit was caked with mud as were my boots. I must have been a sorry spectacle as I ran through the farmyard towards a building that had a door in two halves. The bottom half was closed but the top was open so I tumbled over the closed half rather than waste time in fumbling with the lock. All hell was let loose. I had tumbled into a pigsty and my sudden arrival disturbed the piglets who began to squeal unmercifully and crash around the room. I pressed myself against the door and decided it was time to leave. As I turned to get out I saw an elderly man coming across the yard, obviously with the intention of investigating the cause of the commotion. Imagine his surprise when the head of a man dressed in a brown fur jacket appeared above the door. With a gasp of astonishment he pulled up short. In my best schoolboy French I muttered, very haltingly, "Je suis Anglais". He nodded his head and by speech and signs asked if I was hurt. I answered in the negative but asked for a drink and something to eat. He told me to wait and he returned to the house, to reappear with a pan in which there was liquid something akin to drinking chocolate. At the same time two women came into the yard and began to shriek. The man told me that he would like to help, but that his wife and daughter were afraid. I saw that it was dangerous to remain, so thanking him for the drink, I circumnavigated the agitated ladies and made for the road. I turned left, still not knowing where I was, only too anxious to put as much distance between the farm and myself as quickly as possible. I remember looking at my watch and seeing that it was 7.45, and at last remembered that I had my escape kit still unopened. I was also conscious of the need to discard my outer flying clothes so as not to be a 'freak'. There was still nobody about, so I pulled off my jacket, trousers and scarf and stuffed them into a ditch that ran beside the road. I then tucked my battle dress trousers over my flying boots, took off my tunic and turned it inside out.

I was faced with a dilemma now. I could not do anything about my clothing even if I wanted to. I also had in the back of my mind that I must retain my uniform or, if I was captured which seemed highly likely, I could be taken for a spy and receive the penalty meted out to such a person. I had a white polo neck sweater that all aircrew wore, and thus attired I set off to walk. I had kept my escape kit and this I now opened to discover several small squares of 'Ovaltine' type sweets, each was supposed to be sufficient to keep one going for a certain time. I remember that there was a 'brick' of chocolate, some milk in a tube and some silken handkerchiefs on which were printed the major contour maps of the area over which we had been flying. The tablets I munched like sweets. I do not deny that they may have had energy giving qualities, but what I needed was a good square meal and a place to lay up in for a while. I still was unsure of my whereabouts, and I had made up my mind that the best plan of action would be to head towards the channel ports and there possibly find a way of getting a boat to travel the odd twenty or so miles back to England. This was of course an impossible pipe dream, but as it turned out the decision to go northward paid handsome dividends.

It was Sunday morning and as I traversed the country lane I could hear the peal of the church bells calling worshippers to early service. There is something very eerie about the sound of bells reaching one's ears and it brought back to me memories of my childhood, when in our small town the parish church bells rang out with a similar message. My mind was thus occupied when I saw a small girl coming along the road towards me pushing what seemed to be a small wheelbarrow. I realised at once that I had no alternative but to pass her, and made up my mind to ask her the name of the town I could see in the distance on my right. In my halting French I bid her good morning and asked her to tell me the name of the town. She answered, not the least bit perturbed, that it was Chauny. I thanked her and resumed my walking. It was at this point that I was aware that I had been indiscreet in speaking to the child, but I had the impression that she was not the slightest bit scared or suspicious and possibly had taken me for a German soldier. Now that I knew where I was I decided to retreat into the fields to a copse of trees, there to have a rest, look at my sketchy maps and see if any interest had been aroused by the little girl. The encounter had done wonders for my confidence, and I decided that perhaps the best plan of campaign would be to stick to the minor roads, walk during the day and try to get a bed for the night. It was obvious that some kind of curfew would be imposed, and it would be foolish to be abroad during the hours of darkness because there was more likelihood of being stopped and questioned. I was in a sheltered spot and having munched a few more tablets I tried to break my block of chocolate. This proved to be an impossible task, and even my teeth could make little impression as I tried to scrape some chocolate by clenching them over the corner. I gave it up as a bad job and had a sleep.

I awoke feeling stiff and cold, and desperate for a drink. The tablets and chocolate had given me a thirst that I ached to slake. I felt that the only chance I had of doing so was to find a friendly house and ask for help. Here again I had made up my mind that I would call on isolated farms so as to be in a better position to make my escape should the occupants be unhelpful. Rising I returned to the road and walked toward a small farmstead that I could see ahead in the gloom. The day was drawing to an end, and I felt that it was getting colder too. I approached the door and knocked. The door was opened by a young boy and I saw that he was being followed by a lady. I saw no purpose in not coming straight to the point so I said that I was English and would be grateful for a drink. Furtively the lady looked over my shoulder to see if I was alone. Seeing that I was she beckoned me to enter. I recounted how I was in the position that made me a vagrant and she immediately said that she would give me a meal, but that I could not stay in the house all night. I could however sleep in an outhouse, and she would call me early next morning so that I could be on my way before any of the farm workers arrived. Just to sit by the fire and talk was very consoling, but she soon had a meal of bacon and eggs and coffee, followed by a glass of cognac. I was no drinker but I must say that the cognac was like nectar and warmed the very cockles of my heart. The husband came in whilst I was eating and in conversation I gathered that I was in Neuflieux and that the next town of any importance was Ham. I outlined my intention of going northward in the hope of reaching Calais, but this was greeted with looks of scepticism. According to my hosts there were a number of German camps in the area, and certainly I was in great danger if I did not obtain some covering for my uniform. They could not help me in this matter because they were all small people and any clothes that they may have had would certainly not have fitted my six foot frame. I was advised that after Ham I was to make for Péronne, then Bapaume and Arras. My helpers were of the opinion that Arras was likely to be the most dangerous area, and they were not

43

hopeful that I could make progress beyond that town, even if I managed to reach it. I was aware of the danger they were in because of the help they were giving me so I resolved not to add to it by asking too many questions about them or their family. In the eventuality of my being caught the less I knew, then the less I was in danger of divulging.

I started trying in my schoolboy French to tell them how we in Britain were taking the war, and how the Allies were at last getting stronger and inflicting losses on the Germans on a scale that had hitherto been impossible. They seemed much heartened by that, and more so since the drone of aircraft overhead, in increasing numbers, indicated that the RAF was more active. I was able to have a good wash and was given a scarf and a pair of woollen gloves into which I could just squeeze my hands. I had divested myself of my flying boots, and found that my feet were wet and the skin quite wrinkled. One of the problems in the future would be the inner socks that I had over my socks. These were wired and when plugged into the aircraft's circuit held a small electrical current and warmed the feet. I could not now discard them as if I had done so then the boots would have been far too big and a resultant chafing would damage the skin and cause blisters. I would just have to manage as best I could. It was about nine o'clock when, after a hot drink I was taken outside to the outhouse and was given a bed of straw. I was reminded that sometimes German soldiers were in the habit of coming to farms in the night, looking for food mainly, and that I was to remain in the outbuilding until I was bidden to come out by one of the family. I nestled into the hay, and with the blanket I had been given, dropped into a sound sleep.

The night passed all too quickly and I was awoken by a voice calling "M'sieur". I rose, brushed off the hay and followed my caller into the house in the darkness. I was

44

given a simple breakfast, and with many expressions of thanks from me, and good luck from them, I set out once more feeling a little better. At least I was clean and now knew that the majority of French people would help if they could. I had learned of course of the deportation of the fitter young men, presumably to Germany, and visits from the Germans were always dreaded. My thoughts were very profound as I walked along. My religious training and faith was being severely tested and yet it was this belief in divine help that seemed to offer a way of overcoming my difficulties. Along the road I went passing through small clusters of houses, mostly farmsteads, nodding to farmers as they passed me by on their carts, resting from time to time in some sheltered spot just off the road, and then resuming my journey. I had refused to take food that was offered at Neuflieux, and I was beginning to think that that was a mistake, as all I had to sustain me that day was raw vegetables from the fields, sugar-beet in particular and some kale-like greens. This was very unpalatable but worse still had a bad effect on my stomach and was very inconvenient to be polite and put it mildly. Towards nightfall I was approaching open ground again, and spotted an isolated barn some few hundred yards from the road. I made for this and, climbing into the hay began my enforced rest until daybreak. I say enforced because I felt that I would have liked to continue my journey, but it was prudent to be off the road before it was dark.

The next morning I was quickly away, and at about 9 a.m. found myself nearing a small group of dwellings. I turned into the 'street' and saw a man sweeping the road. He had a small wheelbarrow, a shovel and some other tools, brushes and a sickle I think. He eyed me with a curious look and so I determined that the best course of action was to speak to him. I told him that I was English, and asked if

45

there were any Germans in the vicinity. As I spoke he showed no signs of panic but certainly looked me over, and a sorry sight I must have been in my RAF trousers and once white polo necked sweater. Then there was the battle dress tunic which I had slung over my shoulder. Despite this he gave me a brush and indicated that I should assist him in his work. My jacket was put with his coat over the handles of the barrow, and brushing, shovelling and pushing we made our way to the first house in sight, a matter of a few yards. Here he indicated that we were to go into the yard via the double gates, and once inside he motioned me to follow him into the house. He was evidently well known, because his presence seemed to be a common occurrence, and the only looks of surprise were as I followed him into the house.

There was a lady serving a breakfast meal to a man and a younger boy. My companion quickly announced my identity, and the two males rose. I began to feel a bit uneasy, especially as after some very quick conversation, the gist of which I failed to understand, to the command "Allez, vite" the younger man left the house. I was of the impression that he had possibly gone to denounce me and so I made to follow him out. My companion restrained me however, and slowly spoke to me saying that the man had gone to get a friend who would be able to help me. I felt reassured to a degree but still apprehensive, but I realised that I had no chance of escape and might just as well accept the food and drink that was now offered to me. Whilst I was eating I was questioned as to where I had been shot down, what had happened to my crewmates, had I any maps and how did I think I could get back to England. These rapid fire questions were very disconcerting, and I found myself being very cautious and feigning not to fully understand what was being said, even though the conversation was very slow, deliberate and punctuated with much gesticulation. Soon the door opened and in came the young man with a Curé who, on making the sign of the cross shook hands with all present and sat down beside me. He had a smattering of English and so between us we were able to converse in a manner that left no misunderstandings through the problem of language.

He asked me what my plans were, and on my relating my intention of getting to Calais he shook his head and said that that would be impossible. He was not able to suggest another way of escape, and so he said that he would try to give me advice on the journey ahead. A small map was produced, the kind of print that was put on to the back of a callendar, and from this he began to explain my best route and what he knew of the towns ahead. He said that he could assist me in getting to Ham, and that the next town, Péronne, was very full of German soldiers. Indeed he knew that there was a large Mechanical Transport Unit there, and that I might have some danger and would need to be calm and assured when going through the town because I would inevitably meet enemy soldiers, either singly or in numbers, walking or being transported. I gathered that the side road on which this farmstead stood, very shortly ahead joined the major road to Ham, and he said that he and I would leave the present house, cycle a short way ahead to his 'manse', where I would leave my cycle and continue on my way. He then asked if he could use the telephone, and I saw him lift the receiver and felt a chill running down my spine. After a short conversation he came back and said that he had spoken to a 'friend' who worked in a quarry that was a little way along the road to Ham. He had arranged for me to walk past the quarry entrance and a lorry would come out, going towards Ham, and it would stop and give me a lift. Consultation took place with the rest of the house, the result of which was that an overcoat was brought to me, and to my

47

relief it fitted very well. I was told that I would be safer wearing this article of clothing, and despite my protestations I was made to take it. Truthfully I was glad to have it, for at least it afforded some protection against the cold weather and certainly masked my uniform, the tunic of which I could now wear, and with my scarf round my neck the only discernible items of uniform were my trousers and of course my clumsy flying boots tucked into them. At least the calfs of my legs were hidden a little because the coat was very long. I was to be very grateful for this gift, and it saw me right through my journey home. One regret they had was that they were not able to give me suitably sized shoes. I took size ten and my feet were too large for any footwear they might have. This was a little worrying because the chafing boots were causing me a little bit of discomfort, and my feet were getting sore.

I thanked my benefactors and left on the cycle, accompanied by the Curé. It had been some time since I had ridden a bicycle, and the frame of this one was not exactly tailor made, however, after a few wobbles, I was in command of my machine and we made steady progress for the half mile or so to the house of my companion. I recall that it was afternoon as we alighted and we entered the 'manse'. Sparsely furnished and with many religious emblems, statues and books, there was no other occupant but it was pointed out that people were in the habit of calling unannounced and so it was not possible for me to stay. With a blessing I thanked my host, and returned to the road. I was, for the first time, happy in my clothing. I now had a 'disguise' that could be taken off to reveal my uniform in the event of being captured, and it was strange the reassurance this thought gave me. I was beginning to be despondent and I had at the back of my mind that all I could do was to stay free as long as I possibly could, my optimism in believing that I could

On the right of the picture is Capt. Richard Adams (Dick) of the USAF, who with Lt. Trost, Louise Letorey and the author was to experience such misfortune later as a result of frostbite incurred when travelling through the Pyrenees. His two companions passed through the mountains unscathed.

Dick and his companions again, this time in Nice. The Italian soldiers did not realise that they were posing with the 'enemy'. The lady in the photograph was a very active resistance worker.

Entente Cordiale – RAF and FFI

The first photograph was taken in a stone kiosk in Lille and was
affixed to the Identity Card forged for the author by the resistance
movement. The author's 'nom de guerre' was Cyrille Jules Delanoire.
Occupation: Mecanicien en machines agricoles. Ne a Lille: Place
de la Concorde. This occupation meant the holder travelling quite
extensively and would tend to explain why he was away from the
region of Lille as stamped on the passport. Being employed in
agriculture would also explain to some extent why a young man
was not available for 'war connected' work. The second photograph
was taken after the author reached UK, still wearing the coat 'given'
to him in France but having lost the haggard and haunted look.

Mme Hernet

Pierre Hernet

The homestead of Mme Hernet, Claire and her son, Pierre, which
afforded shelter and safety to the author when passing through
Bouchavesnes en route for Arras. The picture, taken in the 1950s,
shows the rectangular courtyard. The houses opposite and the long
low building adjacent to the farm are new since 1942.

The author's railway ticket for the journey from Toulouse to
Bergerac. The cost was 165 Francs.

Tram ticket for journey in Nice and Metro ticket for a
journey in Paris.

Tram tickets for journeys in Marseille and Lille.

Railway tickets for journeys taken by train; on the 9th January
1943 a booked seat on the train from Lyon to Toulouse. While on
the 23rd January the author travelled from Marseille to Nice.

Lucille Philippe, taken in October 1945. A wonder-
fully brave person and the contact that brought the
author into the safety of the resistance movement.
Like her compatriots she never flinched even in the
moments of dire peril, and paid scant regard for
her own safety. In this she had the support of her
parents who were also heavily involved in the helping
to safety of Allied personnel, using their home in
Arras as a refuge for those 'on the run'.

Mr A. Richards, an Englishman born in 1878, who was
residing in Lille in the years before the war. He was known
to my friends in Warlus and Mons Hanot went to visit him to
seek his help in getting me back home. After all, an Englishman would not refuse to help, surely. Alas he did — at least
to Mons Hanot.

The author met Mr Richards after the war and found that
he had been involved in resistance work during the war. He
had been under scrutiny by the Germans and had been
arrested several times, having to suffer solitary confinement.

He 'refused' to help and this made the author's Warlus
friends a little bitter, but of course he set the wheels in
motion for the 'underground' to contact the author. He was
a very brave man, but like many in those troubled times, was
misunderstood because of the necessity for him to conceal
his real self and sympathy.

Mons and Mme Biguet, the Mayor, and daughter-in-law. The photograph taken after the war.

In happier times, 1958, taken with Gilbert on the tractor. Bottom right, with cap, is Mons Rene Hanot whom the author met as he turned from Arras.

get back to the UK was waning with each aquaintance who voiced pessimism at the thought.

What happened to the agreed plan I will never know. I walked as instructed and eventually came to the quarry but I was never overtaken by any lorry and had to find my own way to Ham. One incident that did strike fear into my heart was when a motor cycle and sidecar, driven by two German soldiers passed me, and then I heard it throttle back and return slowly behind me. Fortunately I made no attempt to look around and it came abreast of me and slowly continued on its way back towards Ham. I am confident that my strategy of walking on the road was my saviour here, as no doubt the Germans were of the opinion that as I was walking openly towards the town then I must have had some right to do so. Had I shown any signs of alarm I am sure that I would have been stopped, and then of course the game would have been up. Some game! It was getting dusky and I knew that I had to find refuge for the night. I had eaten that day and been given clothes, so I decided not to press my luck further, once more seeking a hay stack. The soldier episode had unsettled me however, and I was unable to sleep because of the rustling in the hay. I was sure on one occasion that there was someone creeping up to me, and having held my breath for several minutes, I struck a match only to see a large rat scuttle away. It had not occurred to me that to strike a match was to say the least foolhardy. The resultant light would have been seen by anyone approaching, and of course there was also the danger of the hay being ignited, but this was one of the many times when fear prevailed at the expense of commonsense.

It was early morning when I left the haystack and continued on my way to Ham, which town presented no particular problems for me. I remember feeling very cold and hungry as I passed through the town and the sight of the

e

shops made me feel quite desperate. It was in Ham that I had my first encounter with German soldiers, and very forbidding they looked. The long overcoat, calf-length boots and the deep shaped steel helmet made them appear to be a ruthless and fearsome body of men when on the march. On one occasion I had left the road and approached a farmer who was working in his field. Immediately they were aware that I was a fugitive but this knowledge did not seem to cause them any disquiet, indeed they were very solicitous about my health and concerned for my safety on my journey to the coast. During my conversation a troop of soldiers came marching along the road and my companions told me to pay no heed because this was a regular occurrence and that Péronne was quite a military establishment. We were some few hundred yards from the road and true enough the marchers went on their way without so much as a look in our direction. It was plain that I was not to receive any help from my companions, but they did let me have their bread and cheese and a flask of coffee. Thanking them for their help and company I was on my way again. I did not reach Péronne that day. Having left my farmer friends the pangs of hunger were intensified in the knowledge that I had food and drink and so a stop in a small copse of trees sufficed for me to partake of the refreshment that I so desperately needed. I was feeling very cold, my head was aching and my feet getting quite sore when just ahead I saw a small cottage. Taking courage I knocked on the door and as a result I was allowed to enter and found the occupants to be a middle-aged couple who seemed to be concerned about my welfare. I related to them, as best I could, how my journey had been so far, and spoke of my intentions for the future. After a consultation they told me that I could stay with them for the day but that I must move on next morning as they were expecting visitors.

Refreshed by a hot bath and given a clean shirt and socks

I felt much more comfortable even though I still had what I could only think was the beginning of a bout of 'flu. My feet were very sore and on examination they were assuming an angry looking red colour. This was a cause of co cern to my hosts who seemed to think that I was in need of some medical attention. That evening a nun came to the house to minister to my medical needs. She bathed my feet, anointed my feet with cream, and gave me a dose of medicine to dispel the 'flu symptoms. I slept in my bed very well that night and was in much better heart and health when I awoke the next morning. I was loathe to leave but my hosts were very agitated, and so after a good breakfast I bade them good-bye and continued on my way.

Péronne proved to be all that I had been warned about. I found myself going right through a German encampment On the left-hand side of the road there appeared to le soldiers' barracks, while on the right-hand side was a mech anical vehicle compound. Sentries were posted at each gate and to this day I still feel a shiver running down mv pine as I recall the uneasiness as I nervously passed them by. I tried to appear nonchalant and even looked towards them as I felt that any passer-by might have done, and it was with a very great sense of relief that I was past this very dangerous obstacle It was incredible that I had gone by and not been challenged, but of course there were other civilians present and though I was conscious of being very conspicuous in reality I was no different to others around me who were going about their lawful business. Nevertheless I had received quite a shock and this did not help my peace of mind or health. A short distance from Péronne I came across a farm-house and outbuildings and I decided that I must seek help. I knocked on the door and it was opened by a small, middle-aged man I explained who I was and immediately I was ushered into the house. His wife and small son, of about eight years were presented to me and it must have been obvious that I was in some distress because they quickly said that although it would be quite difficult for me to stay with them I was not fit enough to go on. It was decided that I could stay but would have to be hidden in the top of an adjoining hay barn. The young boy, whose name was Pierre, was despatched to see that the way was clear for me to cross the yard, and on receiving confirmation that it was I was taken to what was to be my 'home' for a couple of days. These people were very kind and I have since learned that the village was Bouchavesnes, and that they survived the war but the husband had died shortly after. As I lay in the hay I had ample time to recall the kindness that had been showered upon me by all from whom I had sought help, even though the consequences of their actions could have, and in some cases did have, tragic results. My food was brought to me by Pierre and I was able to go into the house for washing and toilet facilities. The rest that I was able to get was of immense help, but was obviously only a slight respite from the rigours that lay ahead. I left that haven early in the morning of the second day and continued on my way towards Bapaume.

Nothing of note happened on my way to and through Bapaume and after another couple of nights sleeping in the open I reached Arras. It was here that I knew that I was unable to go much further. My progress so far had been painfully slow, in more senses than one, and as I entered the outskirts of Arras I saw two soldiers leading a horse along the road in my direction. I panicked and turned down the small side road that was on my left. This was an instinctive choice and not a rational one since I had no idea where it might lead me and certainly was foreign to the tactics I had successfully employed so far. My head was swimming, my feet were sore and I was desperately tired and hungry. A short way down the road I came to what I can only think was a generating station. It was a small building and on the inside of the gate was a German sentry with a rifle slung over his shoulder. To make matters worse a small dog began to yap at me as I passed and although I walked past the sentry I was more concerned with the dog. I couldn't shout at it because I did not know what to say, and I could not altogether ignore it. It was at the precise moment of passing the sentry that was my most dangerous moment yet, or so it seemed. I heard a click, reminiscent of the sound made by moving the bolt of a rifle or perhaps of opening the latch of a gate and closing it again. Whichever it was I had the presence of mind to pay no heed, and as the dog had now turned from the attack I walked on with baited breath sure that the command to 'halt' would ring out and then all would be up. No such order was given and so I was able to continue down the road, and having turned a bend in the road was out of the sight of the soldier.

Each of these incidents were now assuming monumental proportions, and I was of the opinion that I could go no further and must shortly have to give in. In this frame of mind it was a diversion when a small cemetery lay ahead and by the side of the road. My father had often talked of the Somme and of the many and long bloody battles that had been fought in the Great War. The memory, too, of the Armistice Day services attended by me as a child flooded back as the realisation came that the cemetery was perhaps a military memorial for those resting there. I approached the small gate, entered and opened the small safe-like cupboard that would normally hold the remembrance book giving the names of those soldiers buried there. Alas the book had gone. I walked in silence around the crosses but could find no details of those lying there. Slightly bewildered I sat down to consider what I should do next. The danger of being seen in such an area had not yet fully dawned on me, but when it did the thought galvanised me into action. Rising, I quickly left and resumed my walking along the road. I had been seen however. A farm cart was wending its way from the direction of the village I could see in the distance, and the man sitting on it driving the horse reined to a standstill and said "Vous etre Anglais?" There was no sense in denying the obvious and he shook hands very firmly with me on alighting from the cart. He made it clear that I must go along to the village and knock on the door of the Mayor, which title was printed in large letters on the huge double gates. My friend assured me that I would be welcome and receive help. In my state of confusion and indisposition such an assurance was a godsend and it was with slightly more jaunty a step that I followed the instructions that I had just been given.

The residence of the Mayor could not have been mistaken. It was a small farmstead with a window either side of the door. I approached the latter and knocked. The window at the left of the door was opened by a lady with her hair in a bun style, she asked what I wanted. I said, in my halting French, that I was English and that I had been advised to seek the help of the Mayor. I must admit that as I stood there I began to doubt the wisdom of such action purely on the premise that one would have expected the Mayor to be a collaborator since he would by virtue of his office have dealings with the enemy. Such doubts were quickly banished. The window closed, the door opened and I was admitted to the drawing room of the house that was to be my sanctuary for two weeks. Inside was a grey haired gentleman with corduroy trousers and denim jacket as worn by farmers. His face was of a man that could be trusted. A full grey moustache gave him a saintly look, and to this day I will always cherish his memory. He and his wife calmly set about to make it obvious that I had nothing to fear and that they would help me. My overcoat, scarf and flying boots were removed and I was sat down to a meal. It was late afternoon and soon a young lady entered the house. This I learned was their daughter and they had a son who would also be coming in from the fields very soon. I was very much at ease with the family as soon as I met them, and the joy of the day was complete when the man who had recommended me to seek refuge here came to visit and brought his wife with him. It was dark now, and the lights illuminated the room and for the first time since parachuting from the stricken aircraft I sensed that there was hope for my eventual survival. In front of a log fire questions were asked of how I had managed to avoid capture during the walk from Chauny to this village which I found was Warlus. I was questioned about my being wounded and my feet were examined. Later that night a doctor arrived and treated me to the rare comfort of ointment and clean bandages. He left promising to call again next day and thanks to his expertise I soon began to mend.

The son's name was Gilbert, and he was of my age. His sister's name was Raymonde and she was perhaps two years younger. I was included in everything, the only problem was concealment on the occasions when some stranger might call to see the Mayor on official business. These strangers were often German Officers and it always struck me as ludicrous that the Mayor was being treated to a sermon on what would happen to saboteurs if they were caught. Full of sympathy the Mayor would agree that such felons deserved what they got and wished his visitors well as they left. I was at the time in the small cupboard of the kitchenette adjoining the parlours in which these interviews always took place, and on anyone entering the house I made for this hiding place until it was established as safe for me to come out. My presence in the village was well known to all the inhabitants because when darkness fell many of them would come along to see and talk with me. Mons Hanot was the man who had made all this possible, and Mons and Mme Biguet, the Mayor, Gilbert and Raymonde accepted me as their very own. I slept in a room in the hayloft, carefully concealed by hay, but during the day I stayed in the house.

I do recall that the conversation had dwelt on the fact that some British aircraft had landed near at hand and that it would be ideal if such a happening could be arranged to take me back to England. I was assured that there was no purpose in continuing with my pipe dream of getting to Calaise and by means of a boat making my way home. The fortifications and security were so tight that it was impossible for anyone without the appropriate passes to move around in the area. This being so I was told that I must stay with the Mayor until the war was over if an alternative escape route could not be found. I was very pleased to be with such friends, but the thought that they were in grave danger as long as I was with them was never far from my mind. This fear was reinforced each time some of the villagers called and I realised that they were all implicated and put at risk because of their desire to shield me from capture and danger.

Days seemed to pass by and I had little thought of the day of the week. Life had a pretty strict routine for the family. Early risers to see to the needs of the livestock and to get out to the fields, the weekday was routine. We would sit by the fire in the evening, the family relaxing for the first time in the day, and then after a warm drink we would retire for the night. Often I went for a short walk with Gilbert in the darkness, purely for the sake of getting a bit of exercise. A lot of my time was spent playing cards with Raymonde or just simply talking with the family and improving my French. Sunday was the day when they went to church but I was not included in these excursions.

I recall that on one of his visits Mons Hanot had looked

knowingly at me and muttered "Samedi". He would say no more and since this was at the start of the week I had time to reflect on this word Saturday, and to try to figure out what might be going to happen. Perhaps it was that I was to be spirited away back home on that day, but nothing more was explained except a knowing wink when I broached the subject and I was kept wondering right up to the last moment. Saturday arrived and with it the usual routine only to be broken at about 8 p.m. when we would have normally made preparations to retire for the night. This night Mons Hanot came with his wife at about 8 p.m. and it was obvious that a departure was being made to the usual routine. All eyes were on me for most of the time, and I was all at sea when at 8.45 we began to put on our outdoor clothes, make sure that the fire was safe, and then step out into the inky darkness. With Raymonde and Gilbert at either arm I was guided along the road for a very short distance until we reached another farmstead and turned into the gate. Entering the house I was amazed to see some twenty or so people gathered, all advancing to greet us as we entered. Most of them were known to me as visitors to the Mayor's house, but in the centre of the room was a large circular table on which glasses and food were placed in plenty. It was about five minutes to nine when a hush descended on the company and the owner of the house opened the cupboard door and brought out a wireless set. With murmurs of approval from all present the set was tuned into the BBC and for the first time in months I was able to listen to the dulcet tones of Alvar Liddell as he read the nine o'clock news. The report on the conduct of the war was good and as he finished then the French news was avidly listened to with much oohing and ahing. It was clear, however, that the news that had been given in English was different to that given in French, or so my hosts seemed to think, and so I was made to issue a report on the English version. We were soon partaking of the excellent food that was provided, and after many toasts and a few glasses of wine and cognac we bade goodnight to our hosts and returned 'home'. I was very much moved by the simplicity of the whole occasion. I now knew what had been meant by 'Samedi' and the whole party had been arranged as a surprise for me.

It was clear that my presence in Warlus was creating difficulties and it was no surprise when I was told that I was to be taken to another village where I would be in the care of other friends. It was with a heavy heart that I made my departure from Warlus, and the occasion was so charged with emotion that none of us were able to voice our thoughts. It was impossible for me to say in words how indebted I was to all at Warlus, particularly the Mayor and family and of course to Rene Hanot and family. They cared for me when I was at my lowest ebb, and the sacrifices they made to keep me safe will never be known. Not part of the official resistance movement they risked all to give succour and comfort to a complete stranger, whose very presence among them spelt danger every minute it continued. I have often thought how I might have reacted if placed in their position, would I have so readily responded to a plea for help given by some foreign stranger? I wonder.

I was taken from Warlus to a home in a village called Pommier, some ten miles further south. Here again I was welcomed with open arms by Mons and Mme Jean Roussel, who together with their two sons Andre and Jimmy lived in a large house on the outskirts of the village. They were a family firm of builders, and as such were out most of the day. At night I went out with Andre and Jimmy on walks around the lanes, but there was not the same kind of rapport with the other villagers that I had had at Warlus. I seem to remember that most of my daylight hours were spent in bed, and that my presence was explained as being necessary because I was a nephew from the city who had TB and had come to the country to convalesce. I stayed with the family for about a week and I was startled one day to hear a conversation at the door between Mme Roussel and another female that concerned me. The stranger was insisting that there was an RAF NCO that was being sheltered there. I gathered that Mme Roussel had reservations about confirming that the stranger was correct in her assertions that an RAF evader was in the house. Eventually, however, footsteps on the stairs indicated that I was about to be visited by this stranger

There was a knock on my bedroom door and in came Mme Roussel and a much younger lady. The latter spoke to me in perfect English and said that her name was Lucille and that she had come to help me to get back to England. She knew a great deal about me, even to the number of my Squadron, where I had been shot down and what had happened to the rest of my crew. It was obvious that she was part of an organisation that made it their business to test the credentials of anyone they sought to help, and from her I learned that my movement from Chauny, through Ham, Péronne, Bapaume, Arras and Warlus had been carefully monitored. This was essential since it was well known that agents were abroad who were posing as Allied personnel seeking assistance, and if assistance was given then the donors were visited by the Germans and taken away. This was the risk that everyone helping evaders took but the resistance movement had to be doubly sure of the authenticity of those seeking help because one wrong move endangered the lives of countless numbers of people over a wide area.

Lucille explained that a car would arrive and pick me up to take me to Arras from which town I would go to Lille to start my journey home that would be via the South of France and Spain to Gibraltar. Mme Roussel was given a half of a postcard and told that whoever came to collect me would have the other half. With the promise of seeing me soon, Lucille left, and I felt a surge of elation as I now realised that there was the possibility that I would soon be on my way home to join my own family. I must admit that I had given much thought to my helpless situation, in not being able to get news to my family, and I was fully aware of the anxiety they must be enduring in not having any definite news of me. I suppose officially I was missing, presumed killed, but as I was to learn later the uncertainty was often worse than the bleak announcement of death being confirmed.

I had been in Pommier about a week when a car pulled into the courtyard, and out came three men. One of these was a doctor who gave me a thorough examination and seemed happy with the result. I was to accompany them in the car to Arras, and I was given a temporary identity card and told that that was the only document that I was to show in the event of the car being stopped. We said our good-byes got into the car and my journey from France really began. We drove unhindered to Arras and entered the courtyard of a very large house. The car stopped and as we alighted we were cordially welcomed by none other than Lucille and her father, M. Philippe, who was an architect. Our party was quickly ushered inside and over a glass of cognac I learned that I was to stay with the Philippes until my next move had been authorised and arranged. I gathered that from now on I would travel as an ordinary member of the public, using trains, buses and trams just like any other traveller. I would be given civilian clothes and identity documents and be passed down the 'line' by resistance workers. I received this news with mixed emotions. The fact that I was now in the hands of friends who had the organis-ation to arrange my passage home was of course a wonderful boost to my morale, but I also had misgivings when I thought of the many things that could go wrong when, dressed in civilian clothes, I was to travel as a passenger in public transport. As yet I was still very underconfident in my ability to mingle with strangers and not give myself away. One false move would mean detection and I was becoming increasingly aware of the danger that my friends were being exposed to in their attempt to help me to freedom.

My three companions left, and I remained for four days in this 'safe haven'. I do not remember very clearly the events of those four days except that I knew that I was in the home of very brave people. I gathered that in the last days before our troops retreated to Dunkirk, my hosts had been very active in giving whatever help they could. Indeed in the cellar basement there were items of equipment that had been used by our troops but which had had to be abandoned as the withdrawal reached a crescendo. I mention this to stress that my hosts had braved danger for a long period of time and had given much valuable service to the Allied cause. Though I was apprehensive of what lay ahead the example, courage and quiet confidence that exuded from Lucille and her family was a source of comfort and inspiration to me. I have much to thank them for and can never repay their kindness and help. My one lasting memory of that time was that I was in a very beautiful home and slept in a four poster bed.

When eventually the day arrived for me to move on to Lille, one of the gentlemen who had collected me from Pommier arrived. I now know that he was Mons D'Allende who was an inspector on the railway. Having said my good-byes Lucille, M. D'Allende and myself left to walk to the railway station. We reached our destination without incident and as we entered the passenger hall a man, whom I had never seen in my life before approached and shook me warmly by the hand, embraced Lucille and M. D'Allende. I was astonished to find that the handshake had left me with a railway ticket, and so we passed the collector by handing our tickets. I recall seeing many German soldiers walking about the platform just as one saw similar scenes on our stations. Some of the troops were on duty, some would be breaking their journey and others either terminating or beginning their movement to or from their unit. Whatever the reason for their presence I felt very much on edge and it was only the calming influence of Lucille and M. D'Allende that enabled me to endure the time before our train arrived. We said our good-byes and M. D'Allende and myself entered a compartment that had already several passengers, seemingly known to my companion. I had been briefed before parting that I should assume a sleeping posture when in the train and this would deter any fellow passenger from striking up a conversation, which of course would have been fatal. With my eyes closed I was aware that M. D'Allende was on friendly terms with our compartment occupants, which is not surprising since we were in a carriage used by railway officials and workers. The ticket was not required since my companion vouched for me and I was left to 'sleep'. I was very saddened to learn after the war that shortly after this journey, M. Allende was taken by the Germans and shot. He was a very brave man, one of countless number who made the supreme sacrifice even though he could have sat back and awaited the war to finish.

We reached Lille and went by tram to an outskirt area called La Madeleine and it was here that I said good-bye to my guide, M. D'Allende. I was now to stay with a widow who was a link in the resistance 'chain'. There was also staying at the house a Belgian pilot, who had been shot down while on a sweep over the area from his base in England, whose name was Marcel. He, as could be expected, spoke very good English and so any conversation from thereon

62

was made much easier because he was able to translate any difficult words or phrases for me. I was by this time becoming fairly proficient in my French and it is very true when we are told that the best way to learn a foreign language is to live with the people concerned and speak no English. Nevertheless there were times when local expressions and dialect caused difficulty and it was then that Marcel was of great help.

Whilst at La Madeleine I was fully kitted out with civilian clothes and had a very frightening excursion to have a photograph taken for an identity card. My hostess took me into town and we went into a store that had a photography booth for the use of its customers, a similar booth that one would find in many establishments today. There was a queue waiting to have passport photos taken and when my turn came I was 'nudged' into the booth and drew the curtain behind me. I was photographed in left and right profile and also full face, and then had to wait outside for several minutes before the photos were released from a machine into which the appropriate number of francs had been placed. The photos were ghastly. Never photogenic in normal times the product of this camera showed me as a lean, ashen faced frightened man. I have the photo to this day and cannot resist a wry smile whenever I come across it. However, bad though it was, it served me well and was eventually stuck onto an identity card to enable me to produce the document whenever I was challenged.

It would be wrong to gloss over the production of this identity card, because it was the work of one of the finest men that I will ever meet. It was not the practice for the names of those engaged in resistance work to be divulged and so from now on I was never to know the identity or addresses of those helping me. The resistance line was so important that it had to be protected at all costs and so names used were always 'nom de guerres' and in the event of being captured the escaper was unable to divulge the true names of those who had helped him. I will call the 'artist' who produced my identity document, St. John. He it was that visited the house in La Madeleine carrying with him a brief-case that contained blank cards and stamps and seals of almost all the prefectures through whose territory our route to freedom would take. Carefully writing in all the necessary details on the document he would finish by franking it with the appropriate seal or stamp and then forge the signature of the official. I was given the name of Cyrille Jules Delanoire, and my occupation was that of a mechanic engaged in the repair of farm machinery. I gathered that this occupation was good enough to explain why I was required to travel extensively. To all intents and purposes it was an official document and would stand any examination but would never protect the holder from close interrogation since the language barrier would give the game away. If that should happen we were of course never to acknowledge that we had a companion. We were always on our own.

The next part of our journey was to be undertaken by train to Paris and Marcel, M. St. John and I set out early one morning for the railway station. Again I had been briefed to travel with Marcel as my 'spokesman' and that I had to keep a low profile by falling asleep in the train until I was required, either to show my ticket or alight from the train at our destination. I shall never forget that journey. We entered the train which was very full. It was an open compartment train with the gangway right down the middle of the carriage. The seats were for two passengers facing each other and above the seat was a luggage rack on which we put our belongings. I got a seat next to the window with Marcel on my right. In the opposite seats were two Frenchmen who smoked incessantly and talked as much.

The compartment was full and there were several passengers standing in the aisle, one of these, by design, was M. St. John. He laughed and clowned to draw attention to himself and to assist in our privacy. I found that it was a difficult task to pretend to sleep, especially since I knew that there were elderly ladies standing and here was I, a fit young man, occupying a seat. My upbringing had taught me to always give my seat to a lady or a person much older than myself, but of course in our situation convention had to go out of the window. There was one incident that really shook me. On one occasion the train came to a sudden halt, and the jerk made one of those standing in the aisle lurch into our seats. With profuse apologies the poor fellow regained his composure but his hand on my shoulder, which was a reactionary movement, caused my heart to stop beating and I am sure that I must have turned ashen white. It is difficult to explain the feeling of feeling guilty and trying to hide one's true identity and all the while one cannot help thinking of what would happen if only those around guessed one's secret. Such thoughts were always present at the beginning and when something happened such as I have just described the impulse is to give an involuntary acceptance of the apology which would have been fatal. As it happened I had the presence of mind to smile and settle down to resume my sleep. Marcel was able to assure the unfortunate passenger that no harm had been done and indeed it was not his fault that he had overbalanced.

The train wound its way, with many stops and starts, to Douai and there was the usual activity of passengers pushing to get off against the tide of those trying to find room to stand. This bustling scene was seemingly of no interest to me as I continued to sleep oblivious of all that was going on around me, but in reality catching every sound and being very much aware of the discomfort being experienced by those who were obliged to stand in the aisle. Marcel remained seated beside me and the incomparable St. John continued to entertain all those within earshot with his own brand of conversation, punctuated with hearty laughter.

In a similar manner we progressed through Cambrai, St. Quentin, Compiègne until we reached the outskirts of Paris. This was the dreaded moment for me. While I was sitting in the train in comparative security the rest of the world held little or no interest for me. Indeed the less that I was involved the better I liked it, and so it was with a certain amount of misgiving that I felt a nudge from Marcel to indicate that the time had come to make preparations for our arrival in Paris. The journey from Lille had not been comfortable and the one hundred and fifty miles or so seemed to have taken a lifetime to traverse. That had been the easy part, now we were to be exposed to the hustle and bustle of Paris' premier station, the Gare Du Nord. It was obvious that as long as there were throngs of people about then the danger of being singled out for questioning was minimised but even so the sight of the many German soldiers, gendarmes and railway officials made my heart beat faster than normal and it was a relief when we passed through the ticket barrier unchallenged and made for the underground. We were to be met there by our next host and taken to our new 'home' and so the three of us tried to look as normal passengers would while waiting for the train. I was flanked either side by my two companions and it was slightly unnerving when we were approached by a middle-aged man and a very pretty young girl. They were our 'contacts' and soon we were engaged in cordial embraces and excited conversation as would be normal when friends meet. Quietly it was explained to me that I was to go with the gentleman, Mons Leveque and his daughter, Andre. Marcel and Mons St. John had another rendezvous, and with genuine feeling

66

of gratitude I bade them au revoir knowing that I would be seeing them later when the next stage of our journey to freedom had been planned.

My escorts took me to the centre of Paris by metro, and although I do not recall the name of the station at which we alighted I later gathered that it was in the vicinity of the Place de La Concorde. I stayed with the Leveques for a very short time, but do remember that I spent Christmas, 1942, in a very traditional way. I learned from my hosts that there were some ten Allied airmen being hidden in the area and also a similar number of Frenchmen who were having to leave their homeland because of their activity in the Allied cause or their participation in acts of sabotage against the Germans. It was therefore no small feat of organisation to hide such numbers whilst awaiting a move to the next stage of our journey. It was a surprise when on Christmas day another four RAF airmen came to take lunch, and we had a very happy few hours before dispersing.

It was the policy of the resistance movement to pass on the airmen in their charge to other places of residence quite frequently to avoid too much interest being created among the residential population. I was passed from the Leveques to another 'billet' and lodged with a middle-aged widow. My new home was in a block of flats, and my hostess had a millinery business close at hand to which she went each day, early in the morning and returned in the evening. In the meantime I had to fend for myself and one of the difficulties I experienced was being in a flat but having to make no noise during the time of my hostess being out at business. If the door bell sounded it must never be answered and I can say that although such occasions were few, whenever they occurred my heart pounded so loudly that I feared that the noise must have been heard in the passage outside. I could not even use the toilet, at least not to flush it and so my time was spent in reading the several books in English that were in the bookshelves. Mostly the books were Edgar Wallaces thrillers and I was very grateful for the diversion they afforded and revelled in the intrigue contained in *Traitor's Gate*, *Double Dan*, *The Squeaker* and several others. I read avidly the adventures of *The Scarlet Pimpernel* and mused on the similarity with my own situation. *Oliver Twist*, *Pickwick Papers* and *A Tale of Two Cities* were also wonderful boosts to my morale and the P.G. Woodhouse novel of *Jeeves* was a welcome light relief to my inactivity. These are a few of the books that served me well and when I was feeling low gave me that encouragement necessary to remain cheerful and optimistic.

Whenever my hostess was away from business and at home, she would take me out for a walk to take necessary exercise. We were just off the Champs-Élysées and frequently walked towards the Arc de Triomphe often passing or being passed by German troops on the march headed by their military band, and an awesome sight they appeared to me. On one occasion I went to the Catholic church of St Marie Madeleine and was overwhelmed by the magnificent architecture and the feeling of peace and tranquillity within its doors. I was taken to the confessional box and received a blessing from the priest who was aware of my identity and who spent some little time with us before we bade him good-bye and left. One further memory was of being greeted on the steps by nuns who gave me a number of small silver charms all designed to assist me in warding off the perils that might lie ahead. Again I felt that they too were aware of my identity and were genuinely concerned for my safety.

I was lying in bed one morning, long after my hostess had left for her work, when I heard the key in the door. I cannot recall ever being so frightened because I had not been told, as was usual, if anything unusual was going to happen. I lay undecided what to do, and when a tap came on my bedroom door I simply called out 'entrée' since this seemed to be the obvious course to adopt. A gentleman came in, aged about fifty-five or so and he made it clear he knew my situation. He was aware that I was Cyril Penna, of number 214 Squadron, and that I had been shot down near Soissons. He knew my crew had baled out and that three members had been killed and were buried in the cemetery at La Fère. Three others had been taken prisoner and were uninjured when captured. This information he imparted voluntarily to assure me of his authenticity as a member of the resistance movement as without such proof it was the rule to divulge only one's name, number and rank. He explained in good English that he would be escorting me on my next stage of the voyage towards Toulouse, and he made it very plain that whilst in his company if we were stopped I was not known to him. I resented somewhat being told of this, because it was obvious to all in such a plight as mine that if we were stopped we were on our own.

Eventually the day dawned when I had to leave with this gentleman and we left the flat and went to a taxi rank to obtain our transport for the next stage which was to be Châlons-sur-Marne.

My narrative up to the present time has described my experiences in 'occupied' France, but it must be remembered that during the first week in June, 1940, the French Forces had capitulated, and according to the terms of armistice, France was divided into two 'zones', with a line of demarcation separating 'occupied' France from 'Vichy' France. The area occupied by the Germans included Paris and other northern regions and, of course, the whole of the Atlantic coast. The Germans, in theory, played no part in the Vichy State, over which Marshal Petain was installed as head, but of course their military intelligence activity was great. The hunting of illegal radio transmitters and the apprehending of those who had crossed the 'line' to avoid capture in the north was a regular occurrence. Many Frenchmen who had been involved in acts of sabotage or who had given assistance in any way to the Allied cause were compelled to flee south for safety. Having done so they either continued their activity or sought to continue their journey, often through Spain to Gibraltar, in the hope of reaching England and continuing their acts of resistance from British soil The line of demarcation between 'occupied' and 'unoccupied' France lay along the river Marne, and it was at this point, Châlons, that all the party that had assembled in Paris would be congregated to be taken into Vichy France. It seemed that if we could get away from the German occupation forces then our plight would be so much less perilous, but this was not to be. There is much truth in the saying, 'better the devil you know than the devil you don't' and at least the sight of enemy soldiers tended to keep one on one s guard.

Alighting from the taxi on the outskirts of Paris, we continued our journey to Châlons-sur-Marne by train, arriving in the early afternoon We walked to a house that was to be our sanctuary till nightfall and it was here that I once again met up with Marcel and several other Allied personnel who were members of the 'convoy'. There were several Americans some British and, of course, French patriots fleeing to England.

It was soon obvious that all was not well and it transpired that the guide who was the contact to take us over the Marne had been betrayed the day before, and had been shot. The link in the chain had therefore been broken and we as a convoy had reached Châlons and had no means of progressing further until the link was restored. A great deal of hurried consultation was entered into by the guides and it was apparent that they were uneasy at having such a concentration of 'wanted' men in one house. At one time there were some twenty-four of us in the house and conditions soon became difficult. We had to spend the night there and slept wherever we could, mostly sitting on the floor. Our guides were out and about trying to make arrangements for our passage and eventually, after much argument about price, a way was found to transport us over the river. I gather that at one stage it had been hoped that we would load up barges and then cross to unload at the other side and then make our way in that manner. Something went wrong with the final contract and because our presence was now known it was essential that we moved as quickly as possible. The manner in which we did cross the river was simple in the extreme. A boatman had been persuaded to row us over in parties of six. That meant a return journey four times. We left the house cautiously. One Allied person with a French comrade left at intervals of five minutes starting at just after 8 p.m. It was pitch dark and very cold with an overcast sky that did threaten rain, and we slid into the darkness in pairs. The French member had been carefully briefed to take a certain direction and then to enter a house that faced onto the river. When we were all assembled we were split into parties of six, and as I was in the first party I had little time to reflect on what might go wrong. It was nearly eleven when we got the all clear to leave and quickly we were shepherded under the bridge that carried the road across, and which was under the guard of German soldiers. The boat was in the shadows and I noted that it had muffled oars. Without a sound we embarked and the boatman stealthily rowed in the cover of the bridge. Reaching the other side we were motioned to lie quite still until the next boat-load arrived, which seemed to be ages later. There were no mishaps except when, in the darkness one of our party tripped over the line that was thrown to the shore, and made what seemed to be a gigantic splash. With bated breath we awaited the worst but happily the noise had gone unnoticed and we moved off in the darkness into 'unoccupied' France.

The absence of German forces seemed to take a little of the pressure from our party and as we boarded the train for Toulouse we were in much better heart and the probability of eventual safe arrival in Gibraltar seemed more certain.

On the train we reverted to our normal code of travel, in pairs, and in this manner Dijon, Lyon and eventually Toulouse were safely negotiated. My companion at this time was a former fighter pilot of the French Air Force who had been shot down on more than one occasion and had been very seriously wounded in the face, having lost one eye. He had remained in France being nursed to health by patriots and had played a vital part in many acts of sabotage. I was not to know this at the time and it was only as we were leaving the station that things went wrong. He suddenly broke into a run and called to me to follow, and we dashed into the road and bundled into a taxi. We sped off at a very high speed, only going for a short distance when he told the driver to stop, threw him some money and the next thing I knew was that we were boarding a moving tram-car. He glanced anxiously behind and seemed reassured that we were not being followed and we travelled for several stops before alighting and then walked to a house that was to be my refuge for some days. Once inside he explained that he thought that he had been recognised at the station and had had to make a hasty exit to throw off any would-be pursuers. It was as well that we were unaware of these emergencies or I think we would have frozen to the spot and have been certain of capture. It also stressed just what dangers these brave people faced in their determination to outwit the enemy who had of course now occupied the South of France.

Mme Biguet, Gilbert and his wife and children. Also the author's wife and two sons. Taken on a return visit after the war.

Taken in 1960 of friends responsible for the author's wartime safety before the resistance movement took control. On either side of the author are Lucille Philippe and Rene Hanot.

Willington Sergeant Wins D.F.M.

The Distinguished Flying Medal has been awarded to Sergt-Observer Cyril Penna, of the Federated Malaya States Squadron of the R.A.F. He is the second son of Mr and Mrs Penna, of 6. George - terrace. Willington. His plane was brought down over enemy territory while on an operational flight and he bailed out. After suffering many hardships **Sgt.-Obs. C Penna** he made his way back to safety through enemy country. He returned to this country and has taken part in many raids over Germany and Italy. Before joining the R.A.F. he worked for Crook Co-operative Society at their Willington branch. He was also a local preacher and Scoutmaster.

Lt. John Trost USAF.

MINISTRY OF PENSIONS

Officers' Branch,
18, Great Smith Street,
LONDON, S.W.1.

Reference No. *9/177/ 21828*
(which should be quoted
in all correspondence)

12 FEB 1947   194

Dear Sir/~~Madam~~,

I have to inform you that the Minister of Pensions has decided
that the disability *Effects of Frost Bite (feet)*

on which your claim is based is attributable to war service.

THE DEGREE OF YOUR DISABLEMENT IS BASED ON AN INTERIM
ASSESSMENT OF **30** PER CENT. and you are accordingly eligible
for an award as shown below:-

Rate per annum of retired pay (1)	Rate per annum of family allowance (2)	From (3)	To (4)
£72/-/.	£10/16/-	12th February 1947	6th February 1948

The retired pay is at the rate appropriate to the rank
of *Flight Lieutenant.*

Flight Lieut C. Penna D.F.M.

25, Wolseleigh Terrace,

Gosforth, Newcastle on Tyne.

DM 1052/1   /Application

SUMMARY OF MEDICAL BOARD HELD AT *Roy RAF Greg M.C*   R.A.F. Form 657
Naval Form M254

Rank and Name *F/Lt. Penna*   Number *1500020*

Branch *Pilot G R*   Unit *S R A C*

Medical Classification *S/B to 12 Days*

Date of expiry of leave
granted (if any) *20 2 47*   Date and place
of next Board*   *N/A*

Address on leave (if applicable) *6 Days*

Orders given to the person
boarded

Signature *F/Lt   President.*

Time and Date *5 1 47*   Signature of the person boarded *C Penna*

* Those attending for boards at the R.A.F. Central Medical Establishment will report at 09.30 hours,
or as soon after as travelling facilities permit.

Wt. 30345 01736. 5m. Books. 11 42. H.B. & Co. 51-5647.

Disablement pension details.

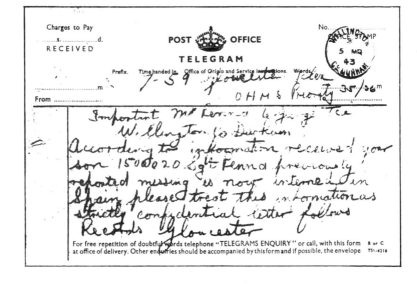

POST OFFICE TELEGRAM

Charges to pay
s. ___ d.
RECEIVED

Prefix. Time handed in. Office of Origin and Service Instructions. Words.
1-9 29th BN/T 52

O H M S

Priority Mr R.J. Penna 6 George Tce
Willington Durham
Deeply regret to inform you that your son
1500020 Sgt Penna C. is missing as the
result of air opperation on the night of
28/29 November 1942 stop letter follows
stop any further information will be forwarded
to you immedeately 214 Sqd.

For free repetition of doubtful words telephone "TELEGRAMS ENQUIRY" or call, with this form
at office of delivery. Other enquiries should be accompanied by this form and, if possible, the envelope.

POST OFFICE TELEGRAM

Charges to Pay
s. ___ d.
RECEIVED

Prefix. Time handed in. Office of Origin and Service Instructions. Words.
7-59 Gloucester

O H M S Priority

Important Mr Penna 6 George Tce
Willington Co Durham
According to information received your
son 1500020 Sgt Penna previously
reported missing is now interned in
Spain please treat this information as
strictly confidential letter follows
Records Gloucester

For free repetition of doubtful words telephone "TELEGRAMS ENQUIRY" or call, with this form
at office of delivery. Other enquiries should be accompanied by this form and if possible, the envelope

Telegram 1

Charges to pay

.... s. .... d.

RECEIVED

.... m

From ....

POST OFFICE

TELEGRAM

Prefix. Time handed in. Office of Origin and Service Instructions. Words.

3-25 London Telex OHMS

No. ....

OFFICE STAMP

.... m

To ....

R J Penna Esq 6 George Tce
Willington Co Durham
KWY 22.0/19 from Airministry
Kingsway P1663 19/4. Your
son Sgt Cyril Penna has
arrived at Gibraltar stop
1230 B/19

For free repetition of doubtful words telephone "TELEGRAMS ENQUIRY" or call, with this form B or C
at office of delivery. Other enquiries should be accompanied by this form and if possible, the envelope T51-5274

Telegram 2

Charges to Pay

.... s. .... d.

RECEIVED

.... m

From ....

POST OFFICE

TELEGRAM

Prefix. Time handed in. Office of Origin and Service Instructions.

1-1-8 London Telex

OHMS 42/60

No. ....

OFFICE STAMP

.... m

To ....

R J Penna Esq 6 George Tce
Willington Co Durham
KWY. 94/3 from air ministry Kingsway P1364
3/5 your son Sgt Cyril Penna has
arrived in the United Kingdom and
has been admitted to hospital at
West Kirby nr Liverpool
031015B

For free repetition of doubtful words telephone "TELEGRAMS ENQUIRY" or call, with this form B or C
at office of delivery. Other enquiries should be accompanied by this form and if possible, the envelope 51-5087

Medical History In Respect of FG/OFF Penna C. 171767 - R.A.F.

DATE OF EXAM/BOARD.	RELEVANT HISTORY	MEDICAL CATEGORY
JANUARY 1943	.Sustained Frost Bite Left Feet and Right Foot.	
25th April 1943	Admitted Hospital Gibralta Suffering After Effects.	
3 rd May 1943	Admitted to R.A.F. West Kirby. (Med Cat A.T B.T)	
6 st May 1943	Medical Board No 1 C.M.B. London Still (A.T. B.T.)	
4 rd June 1943	Medical Board No 1 C.M.B. London (A.4.B. B.L.)	
16 th Sept 1943	Medical Board No 1 C.M.B. London Med Cat (A.T. B.T.)	
5 th Oct 1943	Admitted to R.A.F. Hospital Cosford.	
12 th Oct 1943	Kellers Operation Performed.	
29th Oct 1943	Medical Category .....Proceed.Leave......(A.T. B.T.)	
6 th Nov 1943	Re Admitted To R.A.F. Hospital Cosford.	
7 th Nov 1943	Discharged From R.A.F. Hospital Cosford.	
8 th Nov 1943	No 2 A.C.D. Hoylake.	
5 th Jan 1944	Medical Category - Effective 19th Jan 1944 (A.3. B.)	
19 th Nov 1945	Orthopaedic Specialist's Appointment.	
29 th Dec 1945	Orthopaedic Specialist's Appointment.	
26 th Jan 1946	Admitted To R.A.F. Winterton E.M.S.	
28 th Jan 1946	Tenotomy Of E.P.H.	
10 th Mar 1946	Discharged To Unit.	
16 th Mar 1946	Medical Board At North Allerton ....(Med Cat. A.T. B.T.)	
4 th Apr 1946	Medical Board At North Allerton............(Med Cat. A.T. B)	
19 th Aug 1946	Medical Board At North Allerton..(Med Cat A.T. B. Limited Below 10.000. ft)	
5 th Dec 1946	Medical Certificate Of Discharge Ref F. 2520/108.	
1 st Mar 1951	Medical Board At No 1 C.M.B. London............(Med Cat A.4. G.2.)	
	" Authority Para 1440 (3) (B) (T). K.Rs. Application Per S.S.C.	
19 th Jun 1952	Medical Board At No 1 C.M.B. London............(Med Cat A.4 G.1)	
1 st Sept 1952	Re - Enlisted Service.	
7 th Nov 1952	Admitted Kent And Sussex Hospital. " Flexion Deformity Of Gt Toe-RT Feet"	
10 th Nov 1952	Operation Performed By Mr L.H. Gervis. F.R.C.S.	
17 th Nov 1952	Discharged Back To Unit.	

NOTE:- ALL DOCUMENTS LISTED ABOVE ARE ENCLOSED IN FORM 48.

| 29 th May 1953 | Annual Medical (A.M.O. 518/50)............(Med Cat A.4. G.1.) | |

NOTE :- ABOVE FORM MED 42 ENCLOSED IN FORM MED 4.

1.   On discharge from the service w.e.f. 5th December 1946 was given 20% disability by Ministry of Pensions Medical Board. This has since been increased to 30% the degree of disability now assessed;

Certified true copy Medical enclosures held in Form Med 4 in respect of the above mentioned Officer.

DATE: 6th April 1954.

         (H.J. PLR. CORPORAL.)
         N.C.O. i/c.
         Station Sick Quarters.
         Royal Air Force Station,
         Detling.

Confidential health document.

ROYAL AIR FORCE ESCAPING SOCIETY

MEMBERSHIP CARD,
1947

Name *F/Lt. C. Penna. D.F.M*

Number *727*   Amount *£1·1·0*

" Let us remember those who helped us in our need ".

R.A.F. Form 1924   **POSTAGRAM.**   Originator's Reference Number :—

BC/S.23191/9/P.

To: 1500020 Sergeant C. PENNA,
No.214 (F.M.S.) Squadron,
R.A.F. Station,
WRATTING COMMON.

Date :—

26th August, 1943.

From :   The Commander-in-Chief, BOMBER COMMAND.

My warmest congratulations on the award of

your Distinguished Flying Medal.

Air Chief Marshal.

Postagram signed by Air Chief Marshal Harris.

The author stands beside the ruins of what were his sleeping quarters
in 1942. Chedburgh, home of 214 Squadron as from the 1st October
1942 is now barely recognisable. This photograph was taken in
April 1986 when the author took a nostalgic tour of the area he knew
so well in those war years. It was a journey he had always wanted
to undertake and felt compelled to do.

This latter fact was the cause of much concern to many, like ourselves, who had fled from the northern regions to the comparative safety of the south. With the entry into Vichy France of the German forces came a campaign of identity checks and harrassment of people going about their daily routine. The German High Command knew that there was a possibility that the Allied forces, who were assuming the ascendency in Northern Africa, would break out and invade France along the Mediterranean coast. The whole area became a seething mass of activity by German and Italian troops, and the security checks became more frequent and severe.

I remember very little of my stay in Toulouse, sufficient to know that my hosts were concerned about the situation and the need to be very watchful at all times. I was staying with an elderly couple, and it was usual for me to engage my host in a game of chess in the evening. I had been with them for about five days and was in the middle of a game when one of the resistance movement came and told me that I had to leave with him immediately. We were used to such hurried departures and sudden change of plans and so with a swift thank you and good-bye we made our way to the railway station. On the platform I recognised several of my fellow evaders, and though obviously not able to acknowledge their presence nevertheless an eye flash of recognition passed between us. In pairs, the usual French and British couple, we boarded the train in the darkness mingling with the numerous other passengers and dispersing over the whole length of the train. The ploy of moving when the passenger traffic was most intense was never more welcome than at this moment because the sheer weight of the numbers travelling seemed to ease a little of the tension that I, and no doubt the other members, felt. There is a feeling of security when enveloped in a crowd of people that is clearly missing when

73

one is in a small company.

The train hissed its way out of the station and I recall that it was beginning to get light as we reached our next refuge and alighted at Marseille. Passing through the ticket barrier with the throng of passengers and under the watchful eyes of some Italian soldiers we made our way to a small house not far from the station. My memories of the stay here are very dim and I do know that my stay was short. Again the Allied successes in Tunisia strengthened the belief that an invasion was very imminent and so the old port area of Marseille was deemed a strict security zone and the defences were strengthened to combat an attack from the Mediterranean. It now became highly dangerous to move about without an official reason or at least being able to give sufficient reason for doing so when stopped at the many check points. The presence of the Allied personnel was a cause of great anxiety to the resistance movement and so it was decided that once again we would have to be moved. On this occasion we went further east, leaving the Marseille and Toulon area behind us. I recall that we arrived in Nice on Friday 22nd January and it seemed that we were getting further away from Spain with each move that we had to make.

Nice was much quieter from the military presence point of view. Each day we joined the number of civilians who were to be seen walking along the sea front. The only sign of military might was when a group of Italian soldiers marched by or when the Italian sentries passed as they patrolled their beat along the sea wall. Indeed as I write I have before me a photograph of three American airmen and their French hostess sitting on a sea wall, and behind them are standing three Italian soldiers, rifles slung over their shoulders, and all posing before the camera. Can you imagine the nerve? This act was of course in keeping with my own theory of being absolutely open in moving about, because anything done furtively did attract attention and inevitably led to questioning and ultimate discovery and capture. I was lodged with a lady in Nice for a few days and in that time she would take me out shopping. She was a heavy woman with a shrill voice and all the time that we were out she berated me for my indolence, so much so that many a passing civilian looked at me with sympathy in their eyes. I suppose to them I was something to be pitied as being very severely 'hen pecked' or worse still perhaps a little stupid. Whatever the reason for their 'understanding' looks, I hated being made such a spectacle of. On one occasion when I returned from a particularly heavy dose of such treatment I did make known my dislike of being treated like an idiot but fortunately I was moved to another refuge after my protest, not that this had anything to do with the move.

I was now living in another part of Nice, away from the sea front and in a flat with an elderly couple who were very timid and I was not allowed outside the door. It came as no surprise when a visitor arrived and said that I had to get ready to move once again. I had been in Nice for only a matter of some nine days, but had had three moves in that time. The resistance intelligence was very sound and the move made by the enemy seemed always to be known as soon as the decision had been made. I think that the presence in Nice of a number of Allied airmen on the run had been sensed by the authorities and so house to house searches were authorised in the suspect areas. Before such searches could be carried out, the intention was known and we were moved to a safer haven. Ultimately, however, it became too dangerous to remain in Nice and so once again we were on the move back toward the Pyrenees area.

We left Nice late at night aboard a packed train. Our journey would now take us through the heavily fortified and defended zone of Marseille. I had once more recognised some of my compatriots as fellow passengers although, as usual, I had to ignore and be ignored. I remember thinking how nice it would be to be able to settle down without being hunted from pillar to post. It was then that I had a feeling of guilt when I realised just how ungrateful such thoughts were, especially as our guides must be suffering far worse than I was. Now it was a case of settling down to a feigned sleep on the train as it wended its way towards Marseille. Having reached that station in the early hours of the morning I was nudged to prepare to detrain. Stepping onto the platform I was immediately worried by the presence of so many armed German soldiers. They seemed to be everywhere and worse still a sentry had taken post at every carriage door to support comrades who had entered the carriage to question and ask for papers of those, remaining on the train and carrying on to Toulouse. In the throng of passengers milling about it was indeed difficult to follow the movements of any particular person or group of persons and our guides took full advantage of this. It seemed to me that a strict check was being made of those using the station. Passengers entering the station to join a train were 'surveyed' as they presented their tickets at the barrier. Those who were detraining were 'surveyed' on going through the barrier and handing in their tickets, while those who were not leaving the train were being approached by the soldiers who had boarded the train for this purpose. It seemed that there was no way that we could escape this net, but I had reckoned without the ingenuity of the resistance organisation.

Having left the train it was assumed that we would leave the station by the barrier and so be checked at that point and so we were left alone by the soldiers 'working' on the platform and train. In the darkness and under cover of the movement of other passengers we made along the platform and went into another carriage. I had been given a ticket by my companion which was already punched and I simply followed his actions by showing the ticket to the soldier at the door. He assumed I feel that we had entered the station and had therefore been scrutinised and so must be authorised passengers. No words were spoken and so with a sense of relief we resumed our seats on the train, the military presence melted away, and the train began its journey to Toulouse. The whole operation was a masterpiece of nerve and deception and full advantage was taken of the darkness and the number of people travelling. There must also have been some member of the railway staff who had known that our 'party' was on the train and had obtained the supply of tickets which we used to re-board the train we had in fact just left. One false move and everything would have been disclosed and the soldiers would have had a field day in making arrests both of Allied airmen and French guides. It would indeed have been a great prize for some detachment commander.

We detrained at Toulouse in an atmosphere somewhat more serene than the hectic scene we had experienced at Marseille. My guide and I left the station, and it now being early morning we were able to board a tram-car for our destination. These journeys took a great deal out of me because, apart from the lack of comfortable sleep and refreshment, the tension was at times quite unbearable. There was also the fear that as we had to move so often we would eventually be caught and it seemed that the escape route over the Pyrenees was getting further and further away. All this had a very depressing effect on me but equally bad was the need for exercise in order to keep us in trim for the climb over the mountains. It was now the end of January and since November I had lived on my nerves and been subjected to periods of hiding without exercise at all. I do recall that I was feeling at a very low ebb when having just made the journey from Nice and arrived in Toulouse I was told that the very next day I was to be sent to a place called Bergerac.

Bergerac is well north of Toulouse, in fact a distance of some one hundred and fifty kilometres. The journey was made as usual in the company of a French guide and our destination was a large chateau type of house in the country. Here I found that a fellow RAF sergeant was to be my companion and for some days we lived in comparative peace and quiet. The house was owned by a mother and her daughter, the latter being in her early forties I should think. We were able to take a limited amount of exercise and Jack and I discovered that we hailed from the same part of England, he from Hartlepool and myself from Durham. We had much in common and it was a refreshing interlude to have the company of someone who could speak the mother tongue. I can recall one night when we were taken across the fields to another large house, and there we were taken down into the wine cellar and, with glass in hand, we were invited to partake of the many casks that were there. I was not a drinker, in fact my religious background was such that alcohol was considered to be the vehicle of Satan himself and certainly transport to hell. The wine was very nice and as so often happens the effect was not appreciated. I remember very little of that night but was told next morning that I had to be assisted home in the dark and had to be restrained from singing 'God Save the King'. Apart from the danger of singing such an anthem at that time the quality of my singing is such that I am, normally, discouraged from bursting into song. Anyway a good night was had and I can assure you that both Jack and I had very bad heads all the next day and vowed that any future excursion of that kind would be enjoyed but the after effects would be borne in mind.

The stay in Bergerac was quite uneventful, although both Jack and I were puzzled at the insistence of our hosts in being able to quickly evacuate our room and understand that we had to make haste to the farmstead that we could see in the distance. These precautions made little sense to us at the time and it was only before we finally left that the reason for such planning became obvious. In the attic of the house we were shown various items of radio receivers and transmitters and it became clear that whilst the operator was busy the Germans might have been able to detect his signal and 'home in' on the house, which in itself would have been serious but would have been compounded if we also had been discovered. It is often said that things are not always as they seem to be and this was never more ably demonstrated as during my time in France. We left to go to Toulouse to prepare for our final journey from France to Andorra, a small neutral state in the Pyrenees.

We arrived at Toulouse late in the evening and it was with great excitement that we set off by train to a small town called Ussat les Bains some 45 miles south of Toulouse. Jack, myself and our French guide arrived at the assembly point as darkness was falling and we turned into a deserted derelict building that had been in its prime a small hotel. Here we found other members of the party that were to make the trip over the mountains and later as the night wore on we were joined by others until we numbered about twenty-four. There were the ten RAF/USA airmen and some dozen or so French civilians. We were briefed that we would be led over the mountains by two Spanish guides, men who knew the terrain very well. The night was beastly dark, and the rain was cascading down as we huddled in the shell of a building trying to keep warm. It must be remembered that we were clad only in normal outdoor clothing, since the sight of people clad for mountaineering would have excited suspicion and would have proved fatal. I, like the others, had civilian shoes that pinched slightly, a civilian suit and overcoat. I had no head covering and this was to be a source of regret later on. The Spanish guides arrived but explained that we could not leave because of the heavy rain that would have made our progress very hard and hazardous. What had not been appreciated was that rain in Ussat meant snow in the Pyrenees and it was only later that we discovered to our cost just what that heavy rainfall had added to our burden.

We waited, hidden in the ruined building until the next night and then in small groups we left for the last stage of our journey. We eventually left the built up area and were soon steadily climbing into the mountains and had linked up to form one 'convoy' of twenty-five or so people. The method of our travel was in single file and we had been told to walk in the footprints of the man in front and in this way we would conserve our energy. The effect of the rain was now apparent because we encountered freshly fallen snow that grew deeper as we progressed and this made our walk more fatiguing. At the head of the 'crocodile' was a Spanish guide with the other bringing up the rear. When the first man was tired he simply stood aside and let the others pass and then took up his position at the back of the line. Our progress was slow and the effects of the lack of suitable exercise were beginning to be felt, so much so that after some few hours several of our party were obviously not going to be able to fulfil the climb. After a hurried consultation during which the Spanish made it quite clear that those who could not keep up would be abandoned, it was decided that some six of the party would have to return and try again later. It was a sorry sight seeing one's comrades turn and go in the opposite direction and my mind conjures up the similar scene of those who scale the highest mountains, albeit suitably equipped, and who have to leave their companions in the snowy waste. We continued despite our depression, but I know that we all felt very sorry to see our comrades returning to what was, we thought, inevitable captivity. Fortunately this proved wrong because later I had a letter from Jack who was one of those who turned back, and they all made it to safety some days later and in better weather conditions than we were now encountering.

The snow was freshly fallen and deep The cold was intense and we were really inadequately clad for such a journey and it was only the fear that if we faltered we would be left behind that spurred us on. Our Spanish guides were super fit and their speed of walking was making it difficult for us to keep up with them. Although we progressed by putting our feet in the footprints of the man ahead there were times when we sank into the snow so deeply that we were crawling on hands and kn es to make progress Up one peak we went only to see another ahead and soon we were a very despondent set of travellers. On one occasion our route was barred by a lake that was ice covered and the guides considered that we could cross safely if we did so singly. One man would reach the centre and this would be the signal for the next man to start off so that at any one time there would only be three people on the ice One would be leaving the lake, one would be mid way and the fourth would be just starting. When it came to my turn I was very apprehensive. I was not a swimmer and in any case falling through the ice was virtually the final act because the intense cold would have meant certain death. These were the thoughts that raced through my mind as I carefully followed the footprints of those who had gone before. I found myself listening to the crunch of the snow and imagining that the sound was the ice cracking. This raised my temperature but sapped the strength from me and this was the experience of all the party. The distance across the lake was not great, but the tension was and anyway I am sure that the guides were confident that the ice would bear our weight, but that was cold comfort to anyone who had the slightest doubt about that opinion. Higher and higher we climbed and weaker and weaker we became. The guides cajoled us with optimistic statements that the worst was behind us and that soon the light at the end of the tunnel, so to speak, would be reached. This optimism fell largely on stony ground as we became more and more despondent and disheartened by the sight of another peak just ahead. We were woefully short of food and to slake our thirst we scooped up handfuls of snow, the swallowing of which did no good to our stomachs. I can still remember the snow became more bitter as we ascended and a number of the party were having difficulty with the inadequate footwear we had. It was very evident, too, that the guides were determined that they would get out of the mountains alive, and that if any of us were incapable of keeping up with the column then that was just bad luck and such members to them were expendable. One other factor that was a source of worry was the glare of the white snow and the decrease in the amount of oxygen as we climbed higher. It was also the opinion of some of the party that we were going round in circles but this was a figment of imagination brought on by fatigue and depression. I recall that one of the Frenchmen, a boy of nineteen years named Louis was sure that he could see trains running along the crest of the ridge ahead. He was very light-headed and it needed firm handling by those ahead and immediately behind to keep him going.

We had been about twenty-four hours in the snow when the guides pointed to a hut that lay ahead and which was obviously the refuge that they had expected to reach several hours before. The sight of this haven gave us all a much needed shot in the arm and with a better spirit we continued towards this oasis in the snow. Once inside we saw that it was a crude shelter for those who in peacetime had need to travel between Spain and France. There were no furnishings but we were very grateful to sink onto the wooden floor and rest. The guides divested themselves of the heavy packs they carried and we partook of a portion of bread that was handed to us. Despite the cramped conditions most of us were soon asleep, only to waken feeling more cold and sore than ever. Several of us, myself among the number, took off our shoes to ease tired feet, and with fitful sleeping and wakening the night passed and the guides declared that since dawn had broken we must resume our journey. This was an agonising thought made even more so by the fact that I could not get my shoes back on. They were at best of times a size too small and with the extreme cold my feet had swollen until no attempt at persuasion would get my feet into the shoes. The guides were unimpressed and produced a knife, slit the front of the shoes from the toecap and in this way I was able to 'wrap' the shoes round my feet. I tied them on by using a scarf that I had had around my neck and I observed that others had had similar problems but had overcome them to allow them to continue.

Our progress was slower than that of the day before and it was clear that the guides were upset at this. We were becoming aware that the weeks and months of inactivity had taken a toll on our stamina while the guides were accustomed to such exertions and had a better physique. It was late in the afternoon that we became convinced that we were not climbing higher but by this time we were finding the pace set by the guides too strenuous. It was at this point that an avalanche came to our aid. We were descending into a valley in our crocodile formation, one of the guides in the front and I remember that I was third in the line, when someone at the rear decided that, to conserve energy, it would be easier to slide down the slope than walk. The sudden sitting down set off the landslide and all I remember was the very fine snow that engulfed me as I was swept off my feet and propelled downwards. The fall was not too great and suddenly I was catapulted forward and found myself lying on the snow. The line was in complete disarray and the guide and other person ahead of me were nowhere to be seen. Quickly the second guide came forward and we began to dig for our fellow climbers, and as luck would have it were successful in finding them quickly. No harm had befallen any of our party except the guide who had been leading the column, and he had slightly twisted his knee. This was a blessing in disguise because it made his rate of walking much slower and reduced him to a pace that we could manage. I am of the opinion that, but for this incident, we would have been in serious difficulties and there was a possibility that some of us would have found it hard to maintain the original rate of progress.

We were now descending toward the valley and could see buildings ahead. This gave us a new lease of life, and light-headed though we were, a stumbling, falling progress was made. There were times when we tripped over stones and this turned out to be the stone walling that was covered by the depth of snow. One of the party, a Lieutenant in the American Air Force had lost his shoe in the snow some way back, and because his feet were so cold he had not noticed the loss. Now as he caught his foot on the jagged stones his feet became cut but because of the intense cold they were not bleeding. We were a sorry bunch of individuals that approached a farmstead as we entered the neutral state of Andorra. We were ushered into a barn and for the first time in two days we felt secure. Immediately the tone of the party changed as pent up emotions were allowed to escape and it was with complete disregard for the rules of survival that we plunged our hands and feet into the warm water that was provided in buckets. The pain was excruciating and on at least four of us large blisters appeared on toes and other parts treated with the warm water. After a warm drink and meal, exhausted we fell into a fitful sleep. Meanwhile the guides had planned the next stage of the trip to Barcelona, where the party was to contact the Consul for assistance and refuge.

It was a bitter disappointment when it became clear that the Lieutenant and a Captain in the USAF, myself and young Louis were in no state to continue. Sleeping in the hay with our footwear removed had allowed the straw to pierce the blisters that had appeared and we were unable to walk. It was decided by senior officers in the party that we would have to remain behind while the rest of the party went ahead as planned, and on their reaching the Consulate they would arrange for us to be picked up and taken to Barcelona under diplomatic auspices. In the meantime the two Americans, Captain Dick Adams, Lieutenant John Trost, the young French boy, Louis and myself were moved to a small guest house cum boarding house in Les Escaldes.

We were all suffering from frostbitten feet but of the party John was by far the most affected. His lacerated feet, particularly the left one, had become very infected. Our medical condition was in the hands of a local doctor, by the name of Antonio de Barcia who could speak no English but was able to converse with me in French. John and Dick were not proficient enough in the French language to make known their condition and so it was left to me to act as go between when symptoms and alteration in medical condition needed conveying to the doctor. It would be idle to say that we had faith in our doctor and it became a source of worry that he seemed to be smelling of alcohol as he dressed our wounds, which he did twice a day often using different tubes of ointment as he did so. He was not a young man and I deduced from what conversation I was able to hold with the owner of the hotel that he had a drink problem, but if we were to seek better medical treatment then the possibility of internment was very real. There was, too, the hope that at any time the Consul might arrange for us to be transferred to Barcelona, and so in the knowledge that our stay would be a short one the situation seemed to be one that we would endure.

Our situation was more serious than we knew. Here we were, four young men in a foreign country, immobile and completely at the mercy of anyone who wished to take advantage of our plight. We were in one room with hardly enough room between each bed to get in and out. The owner and his wife were very good to us and did provide us with meals and drinks and helped us in our personal hygiene. The other residents seemed to be a rather rough and ready type of individual, and I learned that most of them were refugees in their own right. They were mainly Spanish who were wanted in Spain for various reasons, mainly political, their having been involved in the war against Franco. Their lives seemed to be one of vagrancy since they spent several days in Andorra and then went either to France or Spain in search of items that could be smuggled back to be sold on the 'black market'. Nevertheless they were good to us and I suspect that some of the cost of our being in the hotel was met by their kindness. Certainly we had no money or any worldly possessions that we could have turned into money, and I feel that it was this common bond of being fellow refugees that prompted the help we received from what seemed to be a most unlikely quarter.

It became very obvious that John was slowly deteriorating. When the wrappings were removed from his foot, often quite callously and roughly, there was exposed a gangrenous area that was getting larger and more painful. The doctor came and spoke to me and said that he would need to operate to cut away part of the area if he was to save John's foot, and he intended to do it that evening. John was really too ill to observe the concern that was being felt for his condition and so I told Dick of the decision to operate. We both knew that the action was vital to John's survival and so it was arranged with the hotel owner that the necessary operation would be performed in the hotel.

It was about eight o'clock at night when Dr De Barcia arrived with another man who was to assist in the operation. Dick and I had agreed that I would stay with John during the operation because I could speak French and would be able to help in any communication that was necessary. Had I known just what lay ahead I do not think that I would have been able to face it. Having donned white coats the doctors had John carried from his bed into an empty room, I think that it was a landing, that had only one piece of furnishing, and that was a trestle table positioned in the centre. John was laid on this table, a mask put over his face and ether poured into it. His hands and legs were pinioned to the table by means of bandages and while the anaesthetist, for this was the function of the second doctor, monitored the degree of consciousness Dr De Barcia cut away the diseased flesh. I was most distressed because all the time that the operation took John was moaning and I felt that he was feeling the pain. I was assured that this was not so, and that it was impossible for him to have been aware of what was going on, but to this day I am not totally convinced. When eventually the surgery was completed, the wound was bandaged and John taken to another room in which there was a single bed. The anaesthetist left and Dr De Barcia and I spent the night sitting with John. During our night of vigil the doctor consumed a bottle of wine and was in excellent spirits until he dropped off into oblivion, partly due to fatigue but mainly I suspect as a result of the effect of the wine.

The next day or so were particularly harrowing because by now we had lost any confidence we had in our medical treatment. John was still very sore and to make matters worse my left foot was becoming increasingly swollen, red and sore. I spoke to the hotel owner about this and he was most disturbed and when suddenly I was wracked with pain he sent for Dr De Barcia. I was too ill to fully take notice of the argument that ensued when the doctor arrived but it was clear that he felt that an operation was needed and the hotel owner objected to it being done in the hotel and was insisting that I was taken to the clinic. Two of the other residents joined in the discussion and it was agreed that I should go to the hospital. The doctor explained that I had a very badly infected foot and that it was imperative that an amputation of several toes was carried out immediately. I recall that at the time I would have agreed to anything that would have eased the pain but having seen how crudely John had been treated I was happy to go to hospital, even if it meant my being interned. I was carried down the stairs by two of the residents whose parting words to De Barcia were in the form of a threat as to what would happen to him if ought befell me. Placed in the taxi, and with the doctor beside me we sped off into the night, heading for the clinic.

On arrival I was carried into the hospital and laid on a trolley which was wheeled along the corridor. Either my head was clearing so that I was thinking more positively or perhaps it was fear that prompted me to clutch the arm of a doctor who came to speak to De Barcia. I asked if the newcomer was a doctor and on being answered in the affirmative I explained in my halting French that I would be happy to have a second opinion as to whether an amputation was really necessary. There seemed to be a heated exchange of words, in Spanish, between the two doctors and as a result Dr De Barcia turned and stormed out of the corridor. I was wheeled to a small room and placed on a bed and the doctor to whom I had appealed, and a nurse, gave my foot a very thorough examination. I was then told that I had a very bad foot but that, although eventually an amputation might be required, it was by no means an immediate necessity. I learned that I was in the clinic and that the doctor to whom I was speaking was Professor Trias. He explained that because I had been brought to the hospital and had asked for a second opinion then that was my right, but Dr De Barcia had been opposed to my staying since he was adamant that an amputation was essential and would have taken me away to some other accommodation so that the surgery could have been performed. It was a combination of fear of what might happen in the knowledge of John's treatment plus the grasping of straws that had led me to make such an earnest appeal to Professor Trias, and once again fate was with me.

I was laid in a bed with the foot elevated and by a combination of hot fomentations and injections of olive oil, or something similar, the poison was gradually drained from my foot from the side of the ball of my foot at the big toe joint which I understand is the metatarsal joint. It was indeed heaven to be in such luxury and in between treatment I was able to talk about how we had come to be in our present predicament and I was able to voice my disquiet about the condition of John, Dick and Louis and of the treatment we had received. The Professor was non-committal except to say that he could do nothing for the other three unless they too were brought into the hospital, because they were in the care of another practitioner and medical ethics prevented any interference without request from the other doctor. I was still troubled, however, and I could not get out of my mind the plight that the others were in whilst I was in comparative safety. As the days passed and I got stronger I was told that I would need surgery at some time in the future but the need for amputation no longer existed. This was of course wonderful news, and with this knowledge the discomfort that I was having seemed bearable. I could not have been treated with more care, attention and thought had I been at home and I was very pleased to have the young son of the Professor visit me daily. He was about eight or nine years of age and he talked to me in French and was very interested in the fact that I was a flier and had been shot down and escaped to Andorra. His visits were always a pleasure and he brought sweets and chocolates and cheered me up very much.

My concern for the fate of the others was deepened when I received the following letter from John obviously written under some stress:

Thursday 3/4/43
11.30 a.m.

Dear Cyril,

From what I hear you are coming along splendidly. I am damn glad to hear that. Did the Madam bring you some oranges and bananas?

How are the nurses over there — pretty nice I'll bet. Wish I were with you. My feet are still raising the devil and now Louis is in bed. I sent for the Doc at the clinic to come and have a look today. What do you think of the idea.

Do you know that Dick changed hotels? I think our Doctor persuaded him and he didn't need much persuading. I don't care to change hotels and Louis doesn't intend to. What is your opinion?

Is it true that the Patron here insisted that you be

taken to the clinic? That is what he tells me. Things certainly are in a tangled mess. I wish the delegate from the Consul would arrive perhaps he could straighten things out.

I hope that you can read this as I am writing lying down.

Sincerely,
John.

I was now aware of the reason for the Professor telling me why he could not do anything for my friends unless they were brought to the hospital. John had obviously sent a request for a visit to be made and the helplessness of the whole situation seemed to be summed up in his letter when he said 'Things certainly are in a tangled mess'. I pleaded with the Professor to at least go and see the others but it appeared that my exhortations were of no avail. At least so I thought until the Professor came into my room and said that he had been to see John and Louis and he was afraid that unless something was done in the near future their lives would be in jeopardy. He was very much concerned at what he had seen and after talking to me left me with the impression that he was personally going to approach the Consulate for immediate help. This was of course very comforting to me and I felt that at last we could see the end of our long period of uncertainty and pain. I knew that I could not be looked after any better, anywhere, and the medical treatment that I had received at the clinic was superb. I had the Professor and the staff to thank for saving my foot, and I will always be grateful for the care and attention that was lavished on me at a time when all seemed lost and when I was at a very low ebb thinking that there was no way out of our difficulty.

The Professor had not long been gone when there was a terrific commotion in the corridor. A voice that I eventually recognised as that of De Barcia was being raised in a fierce argument and when things had been quietened down the Professor said that De Barcia had gone to see John and Louis, and finding that their feet had been recently bandaged asked who had done it. In all innocence John has said that the doctor at the clinic had been at his request and this had sparked off a row at the clinic, De Barcia insisting that they were his patients and the Professor adamant that he had been asked to go to see them. No matter what the rights or wrongs of the situation the Professor was spurred into action and I believe made contact with the Consul immediately, how I am not sure. The result was that a large American car drew into the hospital car park, and after genuine expressions of thanks on my part, good-byes were said and I was carried into the car. John and Dick were already aboard, but Louis was unable to join us but he had been moved from the hotel to the home of a French family while his clearance into Spain was arranged.

The three of us sat in the back seat of this very large American car, driven by a liveried chauffeur in the company of another official. We had our feet on the back of the seat in front and the chauffeur and the official sat with their heads between our bandaged limbs. Needless to say we were very excited and relieved, these feelings tinged with sadness at the thought that Louis was not able to share our joy. We had been through so much together that it did not seem right that one of the party should be missing at the time when we were being driven to safety. We were assured however that Louis' exile would be very short and that he would soon be free to continue his journey to freedom.

The car wended its way in the afternoon heat until eventually we reached Zaragozah. Although we were not terribly uncomfortable in the car we were all feeling rather jaded as we entered the outskirts of the town. I had a fever and it was considered wiser to have a night stop rather than push on to Madrid, which was our destination. I remember being seated onto a chair and being carried into a lift and then taken to my room and put straight to bed. The others were similarly treated and we all felt much better after a night's sleep and a light evening meal and breakfast the following morning. We resumed our journey and reached Madrid where we were taken to the British American Hospital which in reality was for the use of the diplomatic staffs and their dependents. The fact that we were of the armed forces should have precluded our being treated there, but then who was to know apart from the hospital staff who were 'allied' personnel anyway. Dick and John were only at the hospital overnight and they then left, and I was not to see them again. I have however had letters from Dick who has a disability because of his frostbite but who manages quite well, and I understand that John, too, despite a greater disability is flourishing in the field of commerce.

My arrival at the British American Hospital in Madrid signalled the end of a long period of anxiety and danger. It seemed a lifetime since I had left the burning aircraft on that fateful night of the 28th November, and now on the 11th March 1943 I was safely housed and protected by the staff of the Embassy. It was 4.30 p.m. when we arrived and the joy at being secure and in a hospital where we could converse in our own tongue was indescribable. I had nothing but admiration and gratitude for all the help that had been given to me in the months that had passed and certainly the treatment that I had received in the clinic at Andorra could not have been bettered, but to be once again on 'British' soil, albeit in a foreign land was a thrill that even to this day has not deserted me. It was as if a great weight had been taken off my mind and for the first time for several weeks I felt secure. The matron and staff of the hospital went out of their way to ensure that every comfort was afforded me and the doctor explained in detail just what had happened and what the future would hold from the medical point of view and what the prognosis of my condition would be. He made it very clear that I would need to have surgery to my feet in order to correct the position of my toes that had been affected by the frost-bite and the ensuing infection. The big toe on my left foot was now rigid and had 'fused' in a position where it was difficult for me to wear a shoe. This injury had affected my other toes and because I could no longer rock on the ball of my foot I was flat footed. My right foot had been affected to a lesser degree and there was the possibility that the whole of the circulation to my legs had been slightly impaired. I received all this news very light-heartedly and I was just so happy to be out of danger that I think I could have taken any news very philosophically. All I wanted to do was to soak up the care and attention that was being lavished on me, and to get back to normal health. I had not realised just how much my general health had deteriorated. I was very weak and was a bundle of nerves and it was the obvious intention of my stay in hospital to build me up physically and mentally.

I received many visits from the Embassy staff, among them the ambassador's butler who kept me regaled with the many incidents that had occurred to him since he had been in the diplomatic employ. I was showered with fruit, sweets and gifts of all kinds and of course I was kept up to date with the progress of the war which was reaching the stage where the Allies were inflicting heavy defeats on the enemy in various spheres of the conflict. Although I could not walk I was taken out for excursions in a diplomatic car and my short trips around Madrid made a deep impression on me if only for the amount of poverty and ruins that I saw, an aftermath of the Civil War which has been described as 'no ancient or mediaeval engagement but a war of trenches, artillery duels, aerial bombardment, attack and counter attack.' It was the ruins and desolation that still remained that has become imprinted on my memory and history refers to a Spain that had suffered the most terrible violence, poverty and degradation over a long period, but certainly over the Civil War era. It was sad to see such dereliction of buildings, such as the University, that had at one time been proud monuments and held out hope to the young people of Spain.

I had arrived at the British American Hospital, Madrid on the afternoon of the 11th March 1943 and during the weeks that followed I had made steady improvement and I now began to worry about getting back home to my family. The matron and staff of the hospital had been extremely kind to me and the attention from the doctor who attended me could not have been better. The few weeks spent in the care of these kind people were invaluable to me and I know that my mental and physical health would not have been what it is today without their devoted skill and attention. Nevertheless, as I have just said I had been uneasy for some time about just what the family at home knew of my safety. It was with very mixed feelings that I was told that I would be departing on my next stage of the journey to England, via Gibraltar, and it was a very emotional scene as I said good-bye to the hospital staff on the morning of Friday the 16th April 1943.

I boarded a bus that came to the hospital and which contained some sixteen or so other passengers, all bound for Gibraltar. I recognised one of these as a member of the resistance movement that I had met in France, but I was dismayed when he cut me dead as I greeted him. I deduced that there must be a reason for this behaviour, and thought little more about it then. Most of my travelling companions were French, but there was one who made himself known to me as a Canadian officer, who like myself had had the misfortune to be shot down while over French territory. It was pleasant to have such a companion and as the civilian driver tore along the winding roads at breakneck speed we talked generally of our hopes for the future and the joy of being reunited with our respective families. I reflect now that it was strange that we did not discuss our immediate past, and we did not refer at all to how we had come to our present situation of riding in a bus bound for Gibraltar. I can only assume that we were 'brainwashed' in that we had been constantly reminded of the necessity never to discuss any part of our 'escape' with anyone, and the need to be 'security' conscious had been so effectively instilled into us that we obeyed the instructions to the letter.

I was still quite weak and unable to walk very far. I had been unable to put on leather shoes and had felt carpet slippers over the bandages that I still had to wear. The bus rattled its way and I seem to recall the route was via Cordoba, Seville and La Linea and we only had stops that were essential to satisfy the calls of nature. It was very early on the morning of Saturday 17th April when the bus came to a halt at the Spanish side of the causeway that links Gibraltar to Spain. It was indeed a great thrill to behold, only a matter of some hundred yards or so, the British territory with its friendly guards. It seemed that all our troubles were at an end and that after what surely must be formality we would make the entry into the safety of the Rock.

The bus was halted while the Spanish soldiers boarded to check the documents of the passengers and it was almost with careless abandon that I tendered mine for scrutiny. I cannot describe the feeling of anger, frustration, bewilderment and disbelief when I was told to alight from the bus because my documents were not in order. My companion and I tried to elicit the fault in the documentation but we were met with shrugs of shoulders and repeated requests to leave the vehicle. I felt very helpless as I disembarked and hobbled in my carpet slippers to a chair that had been placed just beside the guard-house. My friend decided that he would stay behind too, and we both were of the same opinion that the only fault with my papers was the nationality declaration, which being British was not acceptable to the guard commander. My friend made it clear that he was going to remain with me and with more shrugs of the shoulders the guards opened the barrier and motioned the bus through. It seemed that, even at the last moment, freedom was to be denied me and the sight of the bus entering the gates on the British side made my lot seem all the more desperate. My companion said that he would see what it was all about and went into the guard-house for this purpose. While he was inside the soldiers on duty were enjoying the spectacle of me being seated in their presence with only the length of the causeway separating me from freedom and my own kith and kin. There was a young shoeblack who was polishing the shoes of one of the soldiers and when he had completed that task he was sent over to polish my carpet slippers. The boy approached and to his credit he seemed very confused to find me with footwear that could not be polished but he was urged on by the soldiers who spat in my direction as they passed by. It was at this moment that my companion emerged from the guard-house, and quickly appreciating the position, he booted the shoeblack's box away across the area. I feared that things might turn ugly at his defiant gesture but the guard commander appeared on the scene and calmed things down. I gathered from my friend that he had been in touch with the Consul in the nearby town of Algeciras, if my memory serves me right, and that the official

97

was on his way to sort out the difficulty.

It seemed hours before the car, flying the Union Jack pennant, arrived. The Consul began to investigate the reason for my being denied safe conduct to Gibraltar and it was obvious that no one had any idea as to why I had been singled out for retention on Spanish soil. After heated exchanges my companion and I were put into the car, the barrier was raised and we progressed across the short distance to the safety of British Forces. The relief was so intense and my joy so great that I wept unashamedly. The pent up feelings of the long months that now lay behind and the realisation that my ordeal was over caused me momentarily to lose my composure. It was in this state that I was eventually taken to the Army 10th General Hospital. I had said good-bye to my Canadian comrade and found myself admitted to a ward in the hospital that was in the bowels of the Rock. All of the patients in the ward were soldiers and my admission caused quite a few remarks to be made in fun. The fact that I had been frostbitten was also the source of curiosity, but again I was very conscious of security and would not comment on my escapade at all. I was eventually visited by RAF Intelligence Officers who once more drilled into me the necessity of keeping my own counsel and I was warned not to relate any of my experiences to anyone until I had reached the UK and was able to be interrogated by the appropriate department of MI5. An oyster has never been so tight as I was and I found myself annoying several senior officers by answering their questions with the stock reply, "I am not allowed to say, Sir." I was very much relieved when I was transferred to the RAF New Camp Hospital and I was once again with members of my own service. It was with delight that I met a sergeant whom I had not seen since my schooldays. He was from the same town as myself, and although we had not been friends, merely aquaintances, we had much to talk about and he was able to give me news of my home town. I also had letters from the rest of my comrades who had reached Gibraltar earlier than I had, and it was pleasing to learn that their stay on the Rock was very short.

On Sunday the 25th April at 11 p.m., after only nine days on the Rock I was taken aboard the converted troop ship, the *Stirling Castle*. It seemed fitting that I had left UK in the Stirling aircraft and I was to return by sea on board the *Stirling Castle*. On board was a contingent of the Devon Regiment and also of the Black Watch, and I learned that it had been the proud boast of the traitor, Lord Haw Haw, that these soldiers would not be spared to reach their homeland. He was beginning to be a 'sick joke' and I feel it correct to say that he only upset those who had loved ones who were unaccounted for. Nevertheless his prediction on this occasion had a ring of truth. The first three days of our voyage in the convoy were uneventful but on the fourth day all hell was let loose. The convoy was repeatedly attacked by German bombers of the Focke Wolfe Condor type, and it was frightening to lie in the hospital bed and hear the bombs dropping very near to the ship. On one occasion we were assembled on deck during a lull in the attacks as a practice for abandoning ship and I must say that the sight of so many ships in the convoy made me wonder how on earth the attacking aircraft could miss such a large target. I was reminded that several of the convoy had been hit and had burned fiercely, and when the attacks were resumed the engines of the ship seemed to be straining at the leash. The news that the *Stirling Castle* and its sister ship the *Carnarvon Castle* had left the convoy and were under full steam for home was met with mixed feelings. It was soon obvious that the two ships were capable of more speed than the ships in the convoy and it was a relief when no further attacks were received. The sea was very rough and not being a good sailor coupled with the claustrophobic conditions of being inside the ship and not getting out on deck made life very miserable and it was with feelings of elation and thankfulness that we were told that the ships were off the port of Liverpool. At last the journey that had begun on that cold moonlight night in November was nearing its end as the ship sailed down the Mersey on the 2nd May. I was taken to the RAF hospital at West Kirby, a hutted emergency unit that seemed to have its share of wounded and disabled who were disembarking from ships arriving in the port.

I was taken by ambulance to a ward, and as I hobbled through the door I could see that there were no patients in the two rows of beds. At one end of the ward there were screens around a bed and a nursing sister and a nurse were hurrying to and fro from an office to the bed in question. The sister, as she passed me, said that she would be with me in a minute, and when that time came she asked me who I was. I told her that my name was Penna and that I had been directed to the ward for admission. She enquired as to the nature of my disability, and when I told her that I was suffering from the effects of frostbite she began to chuckle. I am afraid that I found it no laughing matter and I quickly and in no uncertain words told her so. She immediately apologised for her seeming bad manners but asked me to accompany her to the office. There on the papers for admission I was described as suffering from 'Shark Bite', and I must say I was able to appreciate that her chuckle was perhaps an expression of relief as the mind does boggle at the thought of someone suffering from shark bite. I was allocated the bed that had been screened and soon other airmen were admitted for various reasons. I was once again the target for the Intelligence Officers who took up the role of the Gibraltar staff and reminded me that I must say nothing to anyone of my escapade.

I had been told at Gibraltar that before I could be reunited with my family on my reaching UK I would have to go to London to be debriefed and interrogated. I had even been given the name of an officer who would be interviewing me, but such was the state of my mind that I had forgotten it. Imagine my surprise when the Medical Officer, on his rounds, told me that it would be a good thing if I had a spot of leave and that I could go home for a spell pending readmission to a hospital to sort out my orthopaedic problems. I politely protested and said that I had to go to London before I could go on leave but I was told that this was not so and in the event my leave pass, travel warrant and ration cards were prepared. I was more than happy to be on my way home to my family but was uncertain that I should be having such a treat. It was only as I was getting into the vehicle that was to take me to the railway station that I was told that there had been a change in plans and that I had to go to London before I was able to go on leave. It was explained that there would only be a few days delay and that my family would be informed of the change of plans.

I travelled down to London by the 7.30 a.m. train and arrived in London mid-afternoon. I cannot adequately describe the joy and pleasure that I experienced as I sat in that train and the full beauty of the English countryside unfolded itself as the train wended its way to the capital city. It was early May and everything was so lush and green and I felt that I could smell the scented air from the gardens and meadows even through the black smoke that from time to time belched from the engine as it puffed and strained its way up the several gradients in its way or trundled through the tunnels with a hiss and a roar as it emerged from the inky blackness. I have never felt so safe and content and that memory has never left me to this day.

On reaching London I was taken to an Army unit in Paddington and for three days I was questioned about my adventure. There were many gaps in my narrative because it was not possible to recall every minor detail of the events that led up to my reaching Gibraltar, but I was prompted and had my narrative reread in the hope that each day, each village and town or person that I had met could be identified and every gap filled. I was treated right royally and in some ways I was sorry when on the third day at 5.30 p.m. I was taken to Kings Cross station to join a train that would take me to Durham City from which I would catch a connection to my home town Willington.

I was still quite immobile but a seat had been commandeered by the RTO and I was soon speeding northwards. At Peterborough and York I was brought the usual cup of tea and a bun by NAAFI of RTO staff and I mention this to show that even with the large numbers of troops on the move the military machine had compassion and I was very grateful indeed for the help that I was given on that journey. I reached Durham City station at 11.40 p.m., too late to catch a connection to my home town, but the RTO was at hand to take me to a transit unit for the night and to make sure that I was put aboard the first bus that left the city bus station the following morning.

I had been kitted out with a new uniform and had a kit-bag with several odds and ends that I had managed to buy as presents for my family, and I thus set out on the final seven miles of my journey. I alighted at the stop in the town nearest my home and tried to walk with kit-bag the quarter of a mile or so to my home. I couldn't. I was so weak that I sank to the ground and was helped by a milkman on his early morning rounds. He was known to me and I gathered from him that my return home was well known in the town. I had become something of a hero, a local boy makes good individual, and it was very comforting to learn that great concern had been felt over the news of my being missing and subsequent telegrams to the family from the Air Ministry telling of my reaching neutral country had been received with great joy and relief on the part of my family, obviously, but by my many friends too. I recall knocking on the front door early on the morning of the 7th May 1943. It was about 7.30 a.m. but the family had not had much sleep that night, knowing that I was on my way home but not sure at exactly what time I would arrive. The homecoming was very emotional and must be private, but as the news of my arrival reached my neighbours and friends the house was besieged by well-wishers and the excitement and strain made it necessary for me to be put to bed and my local doctor called in to tend me. I had not realised just how weak I was and in addition I was suffering from nervous exhaustion. It is remarkable just what therapeutic value a day at home has for one who has been missing for some months and I soon began to regain a little of my strength, although I had many times to stop and rest whilst out of doors, and this condition lasted for several weeks.

I returned to West Kirby and had minor surgery to my feet and was sent to the RAF rehabilitation centre at Hoylake. There I was given exercises and treatment that did eventually allow me to return to duty, not to flying but to instructor duties at the Queens University Air Squadron Belfast. I was something of a hero to the cadets that I was instructing and this was reinforced when later in the year I was awarded an Immediate Distinguished Flying Medal. My stay in Belfast was idyllic and I was commissioned in January 1944 and appointed Warden to the Queens Chambers, the residence of the cadets in addition to my instructional duties. Lord Londonderry was the Senior RAF Officer in Northern Ireland and he took a great interest in my welfare. It was because of his interest in me that I was presented to the many distinguished people who visited the University. I met General Eisenhower, General Alexander, Field Marshal Montgomery and my joy knew no bounds when I was presented to Their Majesties King George VI, Queen Elizabeth and the Princess' Elizabeth and Margaret when the Royal family came to Belfast.

I now began to settle into normal service life but the pride I had in being a member of the Royal Air Force has never left me, even to this day. I finally retired from the Service in June 1972, having had a brief spell as a civilian from July 1947 to September 1952. I look back on my Service career with pride and humility. Pride because I belonged to a Service with a marvellous tradition and because I met and served with so many fine airmen and officers. Humility because I was one of the lucky ones to live to see the end of the war and to this day the images of all those fine young men, who like myself joined in the battle for freedom, remain with me. Some survived but many did not and it is with awe and sadness that I have visited the several military cemeteries and beheld the rows upon rows of white crosses and read the names of soldiers, sailors, airmen and civilians who were not as fortunate as myself and who paid the supreme sacrifice.

I also remember constantly the many French people who risked everything to help me to return home and who fed, clothed and hid me from my enemies. I owe them a debt that I can never repay and often I try to think how many of us would have reacted if we had been confronted by a young man lost and unable to fend for himself in the midst of his enemies, and knowing what terrible retribution would have been wreaked had their activities come to light. Indeed it is with everlasting sorrow that we know that many of these fine, courageous patriots were killed for their compassion. Their exploits go unheralded and they received no recognition for their bravery but it must be recorded that in the hearts of many like myself they will be remembered as being the reason for us being here today. I remember with great affection Chauny, Ham, Péronne, Bapaume and Arras but with love and gratitude that cannot be adequately expressed, the many friends of Warlus, Pommier and Arras. These were the means of saving my life and of making my return to my family possible. I have since returned to thank them in person and had countless letters from them. Some alas I was never to meet again but they will always remain imprinted on my mind and life for ever.

There is a verse in the bible that says, inter alia, 'I was a stranger, and ye took me in, I was hungry and you gave me food, I was thirsty and ye gave me drink, naked and ye clothed me, sick and ye visited me'. (St. Matthew Chapt. 26). There cannot be any finer epitaph that could be written for all those wonderful people and that passage of scripture, written as it was so many, many years ago could well have been written in 1942 to describe just what was done for me by strangers that I approached for help. It is to their memory that I would dedicate this book, for without their courage and selflessness it could never have been written.